Textile structures

Textile structures

Helen Hutton

Watson-Guptill Publications

New York

First published in the United States 1975 by Watson-Guptill Publications,
a division of Billboard Publications, Inc.,
One Astor Plaza, New York, New York, 10036

First published 1975 in Great Britain by B. T. Batsford Limited,
4 Fitzhardinge Street, London W1H 0AH

Manufactured in Great Britain

Library of Congress Cataloging in Publication Data

Hutton, Helen.
    Textile structures

Bibliography: p.
    1. Textile crafts. 2. Soft sculpture. I. Title.
    TT699.H86   746.4   74-28497
    ISBN 0-8230-5336-9

Contents

Acknowledgment 6

Introduction 7

Knitting and crochet 20

Knotting and macramé 54
Dyeing 56
Basic materials 56
The square knot 59
The half hitch 59
Sennits 60
Carrick bend or Josephine knot 61
Turk's head 62
Braids and plaits 62
Joining the knots 63

Weaving and wrapping 77
Branch weaving and wrapping 78
The frame loom 80
Basic weaving method 81
Laying the warp
on a frame loom 82
To make a shed 82
Weaving 84
Interlocking techniques 84
The slit technique 85
Moulding and shaping 86
Dovetailing 86
Tufting 87
Knotting method 88
Gauze weave 89

Other methods 117
Rope sculpture 117
Student work 119

Appendix
Addresses of the
World Crafts Councils 123

Suppliers
United Kingdom 124
USA and Canada 125

Bibliography 126

Acknowledgment

The following photographs were
taken by Warwick Hutton:
Figures 1, 2, 3, 4, 5, 6, 18, 19, 20,
21, 22, 41, 60, 61, 62, 63, 64, 65,
66, 74, 75, 76, 77, 78, 79, 99, 100,
101, 102, 103, 104, 105.
I would like to thank the many
artists and craftsmen who sent me
reproductions of their work.

Introduction

From primitive man down to the present day, the act of interlacing, interlocking and knotting threads has been both a task and a relaxation. It has performed a function and fulfilled an urge to create which is inherent in us all. Most of us have experienced at some time in our lives the fascination that comes from handling yarns, knotting and unknotting string (especially from a parcel), making a 'cat's cradle' or crocheting little fancy squares for a bedspread. A comforting sense of euphoria is induced by these tactile sensations: handling the threads and seeing the design emerge as a form beneath your fingers. Those who work in macramé insist that the cords seem to take charge and the resulting patterns bear little relationship to the original plan – as one worker commented: 'it is as if the yarn takes on a life of its own'.

1   *Ceremonial rattle, Northwest coast of North America (Salish). Knotted, wrapped and twisted. Reproduced by courtesy of the Department of Ethnology, University of Cambridge*

7

2   Feather headdress, Peru.
Knotted base. Reproduced by
courtesy of the Department of
Ethnology, University of
Cambridge

3   Ceremonial dress, the Chaco,
border between Argentina
and Paraguay. Interlock weave.
Reproduced by courtesy of the
Department of Ethnology,
University of Cambridge.

Exciting new possibilities have fired the imagination of artists working in this medium of textiles. Orthodox weaving has left the flat plane of the wall or floor, and sometimes discarding the traditional loom, has moved out into three-dimensional space, discovering new materials, values and approaches, to express new art forms. The movement towards sculptural textile objects and constructions, while naturally appealing to the artist working alone, is also well suited to group projects where people work out ideas, uninhibited by rigid techniques and elaborate equipment, sometimes planning a design but more often allowing random free forms to emerge. This line of approach has the undoubted advantage over loom weaving in that by combining methods such as knotting, crochet, knitting and wrapping, several people can work on a textural structure at the same time whilst inventing an appropriate technique.

Initially, the production of woven objects in primitive times was purely for useful purposes, but man's instinct for creation soon introduced decorative features to enrich functionalism. Knots which were vital to such pursuits as fishing, trapping and harnessing of animals began to multiply in complexity and pattern, taking on new forms in allied crafts.

A clear line between crafts (useful arts) and fine art has always been difficult to define and today appears to be almost non-existent. Hitherto craft objects, even when decorated were designed to serve a specific function. The main purpose of a handwoven rug was to provide a warm protective covering for a floor. The designs which later were to enrich the surface were of secondary importance, the additional forms and patterns often being of tribal or religious significance. With the discovery of pigments from the earth and the vegetable world, tinting and colour also became an important factor.

As civilization evolved, fine art came into being. It was evaluated by its form and colour and the extent to which it gratified the aesthetic demands of the artist and those of the beholder. The fine dividing line gradually became blurred and craftsmen began to disregard the practical aspect of their work and to present it as a conceptual object in its own right. The imaginative innovations that we see today would appear to be a natural development of the crafts movement in a world of more leisure, a wealth of new materials and reaction against the surge of mass production.

Full circle seems to have been reached in the field of textiles where objects which are both formally significant and also functional are to be found. In a recent national exhibition, a woven floor-covering composed of knitted and stuffed tubes forming deep triangular units were also shown re-arranged in a different combination as an enormous mosaic, while a further disposal displayed the piled-up units forming comfortable chairs. Another work was in the form of a rectangle of decorative knotting which became a hammock, while a smaller section served as a swing.

This book shows examples of woven, looped and wrapped constructions that may be enjoyed for the creative possibilities they suggest. Some of the art objects are technically ingenious and sophisticated. Others may be haunting and arouse feelings of fear or horror. The idea conveyed is so dominating that one is unaware of the technique. New methods and materials are being used in place of those older ones which are unresponsive to different ways of handling, and a good deal of inventive re-thinking is needed. Improbable materials such as swarf, an industrial metal waste, is an example of a modern medium that has potentialities.

The term 'textile structures' covers anything made from a linear element – yarns composed of wool, sisal, cotton, rags, paper, polypropylene, heavy hemp rope, to mention but a few. It includes the accepted methods of interlooping thread to produce a fabric mass, as mentioned earlier or combinations of these. Related crafts of embroidery, appliqué, batik and tie-dye are excluded as these processes apply to an existing fabric.

Textile courses for experimental work are held at various summer schools, and knotters, weavers, knitters and crochet workers can work individually or join in group projects assisted by professional artists and craftsmen. Discussions play a major part and co-ordinate with practical work on all levels. Although most of these courses are attended by would-be teachers and professionals, beginners are usually welcomed as providers of new ideas. Courses such as these are widespread and popular in the United States. Information is generally available at local branches of the World Crafts Council, a body working actively for the advancement of the craft movement, existing in most countries in Europe and the USA. Some addresses are given in the Appendix. Crafts magazines and periodicals carry advance notices of forthcoming courses so that it is often possible to arrange a holiday to include them.

The skills described here are
simple and easy to master and the
equipment basic: an old picture
frame, crochet hooks and knitting
needles, or the forked branch of a
tree. The design idea is the
important factor, whether the end
product is the result of inspired
planning or a progression of
creative steps. Most of the artist-
craftsmen whose work is illustrated
here have described how they
found a source or theme for their
work or the germ idea from which
it developed. Some of the tropical
plant forms photographed in the
University of Cambridge Botanical
Gardens could well be a source of
inspiration. See figures 7 to 10.
Many of the works reproduced rely
on specialised techniques and are
made by professionals of
international reputation, but I
hope that they may stimulate
thought and activity in a medium
that has great potential.

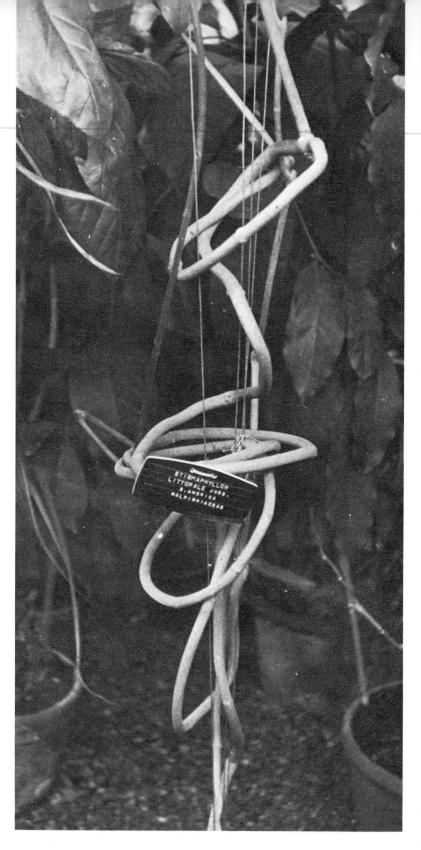

7   *Tropical plant form exemplifying*
linear design forms.
Botanical Gardens,
University of Cambridge

8   *Tropical growth system displaying*
structural entanglement.
Botanical Gardens,
University of Cambridge

9   *A structural skeletal formation of tropical root growth. Botanical Gardens, University of Cambridge*

10   *Succulent plant revealing complex patterns. Botanical Gardens, University of Cambridge*

Knitting and crochet

These crafts are similar in that the basic principle is the interlooping of yarn, using either a hook or two (or more) needles (pins) to accomplish this. Until recently these crafts have been regarded merely as a means of making garments or objects of use, but it can be seen by the examples illustrated here that some re-thinking of the long accepted convention has taken place and it is no longer necessary to copy the designs of someone else. Using only the most basic stitches, it is possible to develop unique and original forms which bring new tactile experiences to the artist and the spectator. These textural objects in both knitting and crochet are exhibited in many art galleries and art school displays. Courses in creative knitting and crochet are held in training colleges, evening institutes, workshops and schools, and have become a recognised medium for artistic expression.

Designing is sometimes thought out beforehand, using the thread to give form to your exploratory ideas; alternatively you can let a general concept develop with the manipulation of the yarn. Both these approaches are shown in the examples illustrated. A sympathetic relationship with the material gives a special awareness and may bring to life a new, unpremeditated form.

Many sources of inspiration can be found: in architecture, ironwork, medieval armour, or from the natural scene of plant forms, lichens, spider webs, fungi and woods, to mention but a few. Several of the works illustrated have been motivated by ideas from these sources.

A minimum of equipment is needed to work in these media, and the fact that little space is required make them an obvious choice for those who have no room for large projects like the monumental woven structures of some Polish artists. Knitting needles (pins) and crochet hooks are the essentials but a wide selection of yarns in various textures, weights and thicknesses is equally necessary for inspiration.

A brief comment on the historical background of these crafts is of some interest. The word 'knitting' is generally supposed to have come from an Anglo-Saxon word 'cnittan' meaning threads woven by hand, but it is commonly accepted that the craft was first practised by the nomads who roamed North Africa. It was later adopted by Arab traders who occupied

themselves knitting during the long hours spent on the slowly plodding camel caravans going east to Tibet and west to Europe. Were the sandal socks found in the Copt tombs the first example of three-dimensional knitting? They appear to have been knitted in the round – possibly on a circular needle – but could have been made in a simple circle with pegs inserted round the edge. Children today make tubular cords by a similar method, encircling the hole in a cotton reel with pins.

Although crochet probably started considerably earlier, the word as we understand it came from the French 'croches'. It was widely practised in Europe during the sixteenth century, chiefly in nunneries where elaborate creations were made. It became popular in England during the mid-nineteenth century, and from a few basic stitches many fancy ones evolved, made by passing the yarn round the hook several times, working many times into the same stitch and crossing and manipulating the thread in numerous different ways.

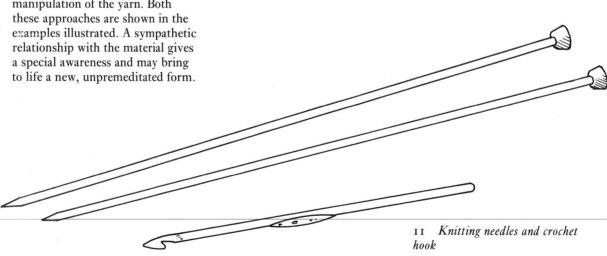

11 *Knitting needles and crochet hook*

12 Polyp *May Gower.*
White polypropylene twine.
A single length of twine,
approximately 200 m (219 yd) long,
looped with a crochet hook.
18 cm × 28 cm × 23 cm (7 in ×
11 in × 9 in)

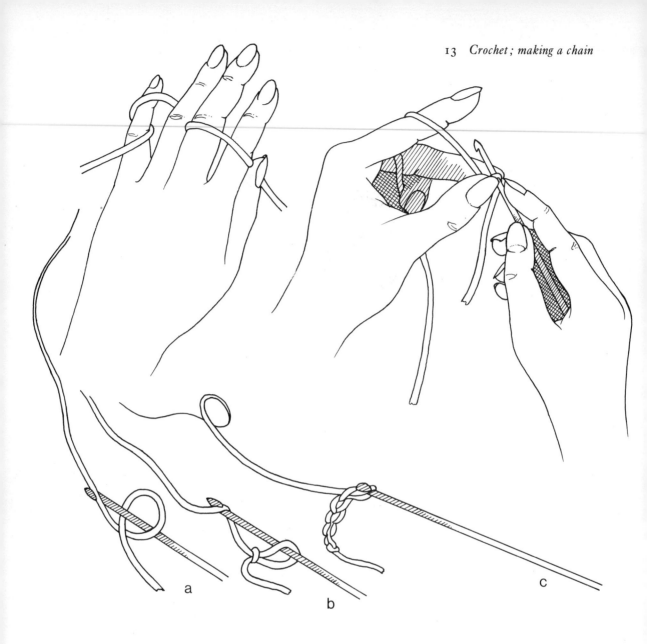

a

b

c

As ideas about form often originate from natural shapes and designs, so ideas about texture may be sparked off by the feel of different yarns. Search out and experiment with many types; each one will have varied properties and characteristics which must be considered. Texture, strength, weight, durability, elasticity, surface feel, colour and the capacity to absorb or reflect light should be evaluated. Working with yarns is the best way to find out about them. All natural fibres have more resiliance and pliability than synthetic ones, which tend to be more slippery or rigid and are best worked with wooden needles or hooks. You can make your own needles from round wooden sticks (dowel sticks), sharpened to a point with a wood-worker's knife or razor blade and sandpapered to make them smooth. Make needles of all sizes.

Polyp crocheted by May Gower shows the use of synthetic fibre as the perfect choice to give expression to the artist's particular vision. See figure 12. The illustration shows only one of the many ways in which the work can be viewed, as it is a rigid form which can be looked at from any angle. In strong daylight the lovely translucent quality of the polypropylene twine is seen to its best advantage. May Gower describes her ideas about working in the following passage: 'I do not work from design ideas. Either the yarn or the technique or both result in a basic mental picture and I design as the work progresses, each step suggesting the next. I was exploring the characteristics of polypropylene –

to me a new and challenging yarn, when I discovered that looping it with a crochet hook gave it extra twist and that by crowding these loops, a very rigid spiralling form could be made. *Polyp* was the result of this discovery. I began with a chain and worked freely into this. (See figure 13 for making a chain.) I used the crochet hook as the tool for looping the yarn to the length of the stitch I required and to enable me to put as many stitches as needed into each opening, but did not consciously use any particular stitch, having no knowledge of conventional crochet and the various stitches. They were increased in a simple mathematical progression to make the whole structure very firm and rigid. A No 2 hook was used throughout.

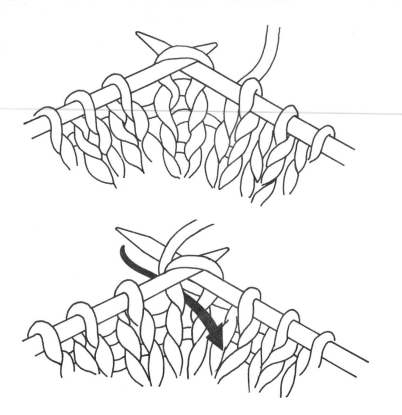

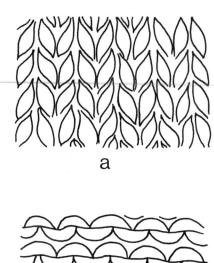

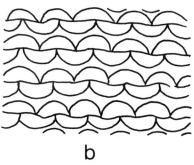

14 *Basic knitting method;*
stocking stitch

15 *Stocking stitch*
a *Plain side*
b *Purl side*

Knitting machines are useful for large scale projects or tubular forms which are knitted flat and then joined and stuffed. They are usually knitted in stocking stitch (see figures 14 and 15), sometimes in multi-coloured stripes as seen in the work of Jennifer Naylor, a student, who describes her work *Dumbell forms*: 'The design idea for *Dumbell forms* came from the pollarded willows growing along the river bank, silhouetting their squat, bulbous forms. The knitted shapes were arranged to create a unity that was visually satisfying. A *Knitmaster* machine was used and the units were done flat in ordinary stocking stitch, the bulges formed by increasing and decreasing at certain intervals. The flat shapes were then sewn together and stuffed. The material used was a fine two-ply wool in shades of crimson, orange, yellow on an off-white ground and was obtained from a knitwear factory as a waste product.'

16 Dumbell forms *Jennifer Naylor. Coloured wools, fine two ply of worsted strength. Machine knitted*

The design for the *Boxed tubes* was also inspired by trees on a river bank, but this time the eroded coiling roots provided the idea. It was also knitted on a *Knitmaster* in flat sections which were then joined into tubes and stuffed as before. These snake-like forms were piled into a cube from which they tumbled, making their own design arrangements. The colour scheme was in shades of blue and clear green on white, and the wool was two-ply factory surplus.

17 Boxed tubes *Jennifer Naylor. Two ply wool, factory surplus. Machine knitted*

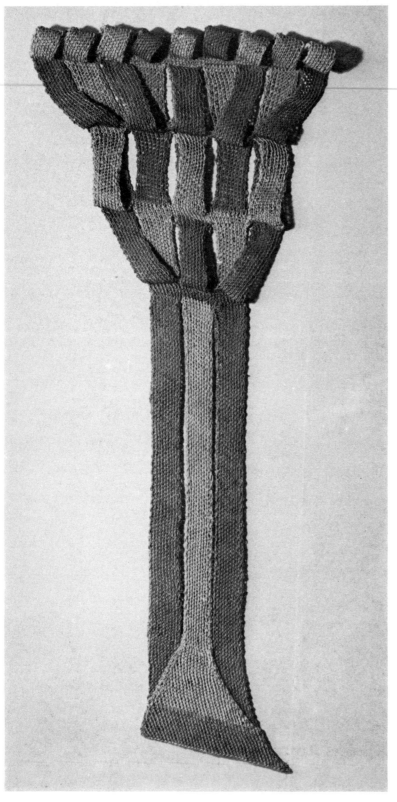

Maggie Arbeid's unique conceptions are in two-dimensional form and are knitted in stocking stitch. The stitches are sometimes twisted, looped several times round the needle to form holes and slits, increased and decreased, cast on and cast off to form elongated splits. Maggie Arbeid confesses that she knows nothing about the technique of knitting and has never produced a useful object in her life! Her down-to-earth choice of yarn is typical. Parcel string and waxed seating cord are cheap and are used effectively. Her brief statement characterises her work: 'I am not interested in technique and complexity of stitches in knitting, but try to understand the systems and orders inherent in the natural forms and allow this to be the simple aesthetic of my own work.'

18 *Untitled work, Maggie Arbeid.*
Blue and orange parcel string.
Knitted as a unit of grafted columns
in twisted stocking stitch. The design
idea was a multiplication of units
on a modular scale, worked out
mathematically. 1·2 m (4 ft) long

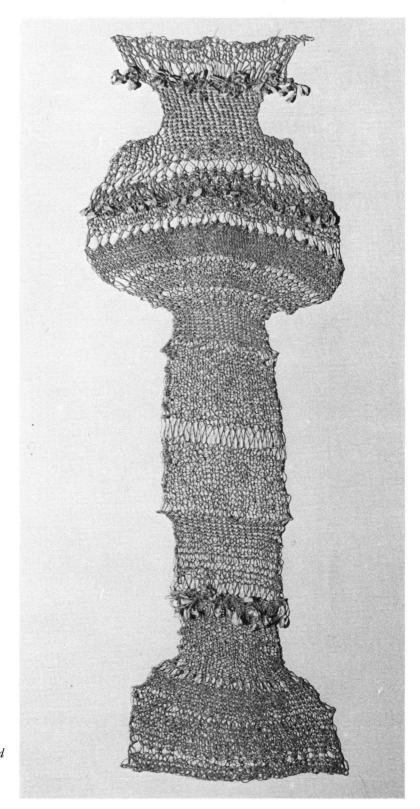

19 *Untitled work, Maggie Arbeid.*
Single ply string in natural colour.
Knitted in twisted stocking stitch.
Changes in the size of needles and
number of stitches are in direct
relationship to each other and give
variation in texture and contour.
The three-dimensional effect is gained
by untwisting string to a flat paper
ribbon and looping the stitches.
1·5 m (5 ft) long

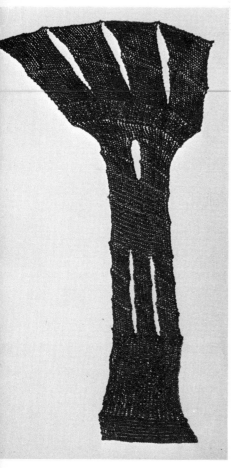

20 Untitled work, Maggie Arbeid.
Waxed seating cord. Knitted in
twisted stocking stitch, giving
diagonal movement. 1·8 m (6 ft) long

21 Untitled work, Maggie Arbeid.
White nylon fishing twine.
The work is divided into columns
with cast-off stitches creating slits.
The texture is the result of increasing
and decreasing the number of
stitches and changing the size of
the needles. 1·4 m (4 ft 6 in) long

22 Detail of figure 21

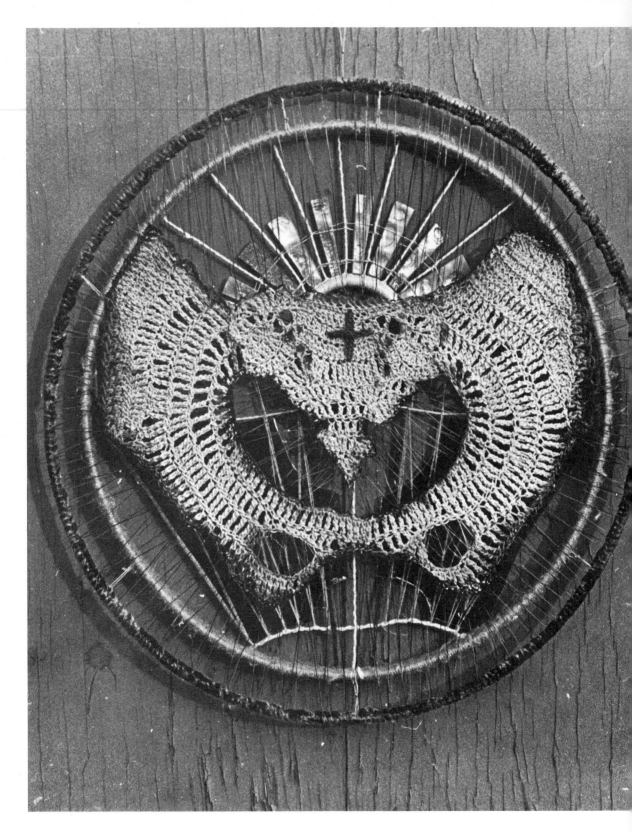

Two of Ted Hallman's woven
structures are illustrated in this
section (a description of his
approach is in the section on
weaving). *Interlaced tree* is a knitted
construction, set on small hoops
and stiffened with resin to take on
elongated organic forms of brittle
fragility. *Sacrum* is composed of
crocheted and wrapped elements
which are stretched on steel hoops.
The three-dimensional effect is a
result of the two plane level.

23 Sacrum *Ted Hallman.*
Cotton, wool, linen, mother of pearl,
mica, steel hoops. Crocheted and
wrapped

24 Interlaced tree *Ted Hallman.*
Cotton cord dyed in shades of brown.
Knitted in dropped stitch method.
3·4 m × 1·4 m (11 ft × 4 ft 6 in)

Edy Lyngaas, an artist well-known in this medium, uses mainly wool or string vest type of cotton in their natural shades. Her work is made from stocking stitch and garter stitch used in original ways. She has supplied a detailed description of her working methods, and the illustrations show clearly the structural texture. The series of tiles was inspired by the richly patterned traditional Aran sweaters. See figures 25 and 26. Edy Lyngaas isolated the twists and knots in these patterns and magnified them. Figure 25 shows a band of stocking stitch which becomes three-dimensional when it buckles up and leaves the background. The second tile (figure 26) shows two stuffed tubes which were knitted independently and then continued on two needles to work into the background. The purl side of stocking stitch is used for the background and the plain side for the tubes (figure 25). Both tiles are worked in the same shade of off-white wool, as is used in the Aran Islands. This is a very light tone which emphasizes the relief of the design, but the weight of the wool is three times heavier and thicker so that the structured effect is more exaggerated. This tile idea could be used in a modular design project as the unit motif.

25   Tile 1 *Edy Lyngaas.*
Off-white heavy double knitting wool.
Stocking stitch. 38 cm × 30 cm ×
2·5 cm (15 in × 12 in × 1 in)

26   Tile 2 *Edy Lyngaas.*
Off-white heavy double knitting wool.
Stocking stitch. 38 cm × 30 cm ×
2·5 cm (15 in × 12 in × 1 in)

27 White tunic *Edy Lyngaas.*
White cotton (string vest type).
Garter stitch

28 Stones and pebbles *Edy*
Lyngaas.
Mercerised cotton and fine sewing
cotton. Knitted on four needles,
size 14. The differing thickness of
the threads gives textural variations
of surface

Edy Lyngaas' *White tunic* is knitted
in the same yarn. See figure 27. It
was started at the shoulders and
knitted downwards, the front and
back sections being knitted
separately on two needles. When
the armhole section had been
completed, the work was continued
in one piece on a circular needle.
Although the pattern of the holes
appears to be fairly random, they
had to be carefully considered so
that the hem would be even. It was
knitted throughout in garter stitch,
and the slits were formed by
wrapping the wool two, three, four
and five times round the needle
instead of once. On the next row
these extra loops were dropped off,
falling back into the fabric of the
knitting and thus elongating the
stitch. The tunic becomes wider
towards the hem; this is carried out
smoothly by twice changing the
size of needle. Edy Lyngaas states:
'I started using circular needles as
I wanted a completely seamless
garment. Previously, I had
experimented by knitting around
smooth pebbles, making a covering
for these on four double pointed
No 14 needles, using a variety of
fine threads from sewing cotton to
fine mercerised yarns, knitting in
stocking stitch with holes. The tiny
cylinder was knitted separately and
fitted on to the stone towards the
finish, covering it neatly so that the
knitted web was stretched taut and
the stone revealed through the
holes. (See figure 28.) This
suggested the idea of knitting a
similar structure for the human
body so that the clinging garment
would emphasize the contour of
the body.

'*Black tunic* was made in the same technique but worked on two needles throughout. See figure 29. The texture of the thick black cotton is a direct contrast to the fine, shiny mercerised cotton. The garment is constructed as a completely flat textile. It has crocheted straps at the shoulders and along each front edge, so that when these are tied it becomes a three-dimensional form. When not worn as a tunic, it can be spread out completely flat or hung on a wall by slipping a rod through the hem. The idea first suggested itself to me when I saw a cuirass in a book of Japanese armour. I decided to make a textile form which could be tied similarly on to the body, thus becoming a garment.' See figure 30.

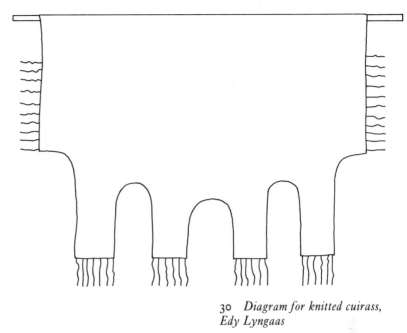

30   *Diagram for knitted cuirass, Edy Lyngaas*

29   Black tunic *Edy Lyngaas. Thick vest cotton and fine shiny mercerised cotton. Garter stitch*

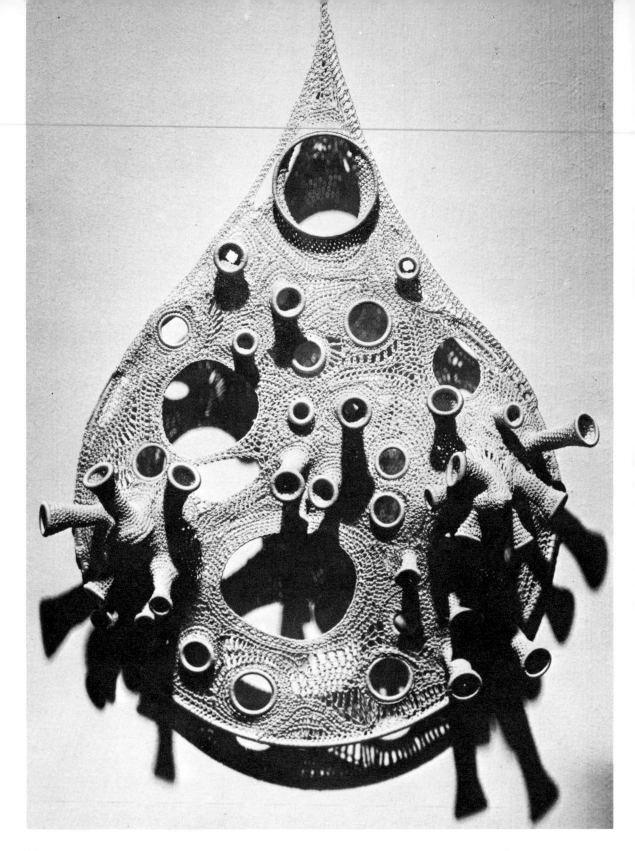

31 Polyped *Eta Ingham-Mohrhardt.*
Off-white rayon on a wire frame.
Crochet. 51 cm (20 in)
circumference

32 Pendant *Eta Ingham-Mohrhardt.*
Cotton, silk and nylon.
Crochet. 1·2 m × 1·2 m (4 ft × 4 ft)

The sophisticated elegance of Eta Ingham-Mohrhardt's work is seen here in the medium of crochet, although she is equally well-known for her woven wall hangings which are in galleries and private collections. Her airy creations with their graphic structure are worked unplanned and freely, transparent and extending out into space. Mrs Ingham-Mohrhardt trained as a weaver, and only during the past two years has moved away into these three-dimensional structures. Some of her works are made entirely in crochet; others are woven tapestries incorporating crochet projections. Most of the works illustrated are stiffened with resin, and a variety of yarns such as fleece wool, spun wool, cotton, linen, lurex and nylon are used. See figures 31 to 34.

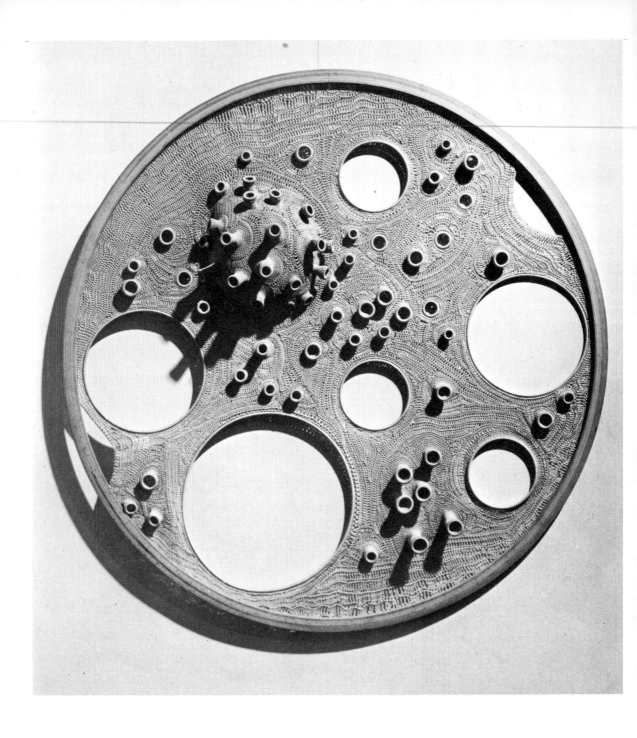

33 Moonscape *Eta*
Ingham–Mohrhardt.
Off-white rayon.
Crochet. 76 cm (2 ft 6 in) diameter

34 Lichen *Eta Ingham-Mohrhardt.*
Resinated fibre. Crochet.
Total width 2·1 m × 90 cm (7 ft ×
3 ft)

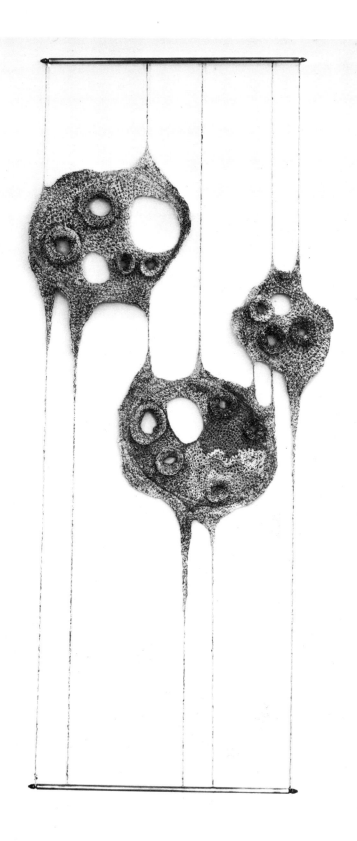

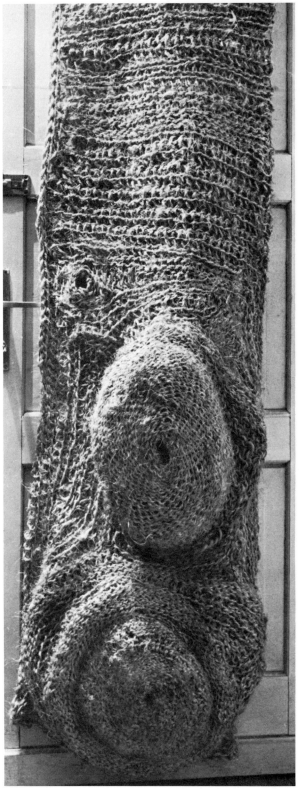

In marked contrast to these are the monumental crochet structures of Ewa Jaroszynska, solidly sculptural and often formidable, emphasizing the organic strength of fibre. She also is an artist of international standing. Using basic materials – sisal and hemp strings and ropes from a fisherman's shop – she crochets these soft and unique shapes with simple round movements of the hook. Her three-dimensional forms appear to defy gravity. Although the tool and the technique she uses are traditionally associated with women's handwork, the soft fabric forms which emerge from her crochet hook make it an equal to the paintbrush or the sculptor's chisel as an art tool. Some of the refreshingly unsophisticated entanglements bring to mind the primitive woven masks of New Guinea. Her work shows clearly the possibility of combining both the decorative and practical values of textile constructions with the more imaginative element of art. See figures 35 to 38.

35   Screw *Ewa Jaroszynska.*
Hemp. Crochet.
Reproduced by courtesy of
Grabowski Gallery, London

36   *Untitled work, Ewa*
Jaroszynska.
Sisal and hemp. Crochet.
Approximately 1·8 m (6 ft) long.
Reproduced by courtesy of
Grabowski Gallery, London

37   Defeated *Ewa Jaroszynska.*
Hemp. Crochet.
Reproduced by courtesy of
Grabowski Gallery, London

45

38   *(left to right)* Stupa,
Monument I, Monument III,
Monument II *Ewa Jaroszynska.*
Sisal and hemp. Crochet.
Reproduced by courtesy of
Grabowski Gallery, London

The student work of Victoria Clarke is described in some detail as it shows ingenuity in solving a set project. The subject was to be one of the four elements and Miss Clarke chose the element Earth. The design idea was based on growth forms suggested by fungi and lichen as being a natural extension of life itself. Magnified photographs of lichen were used. See figure 39. String crochet seemed the best medium to express the idea, and this was carried out with home-made wooden hooks of different sizes which produced the varying texture in each individual fungus and lichen form. When all were completed they were divided into several batches and dyed progressively, starting with a bright green, gradually adding small quantities of brown to convey the feeling of vibrant living growths undergoing a metamorphosis back into the earth from which they came. These dyed forms were stiffened with wire and nailed to a small wood platform (stained brown), while others, chained together were allowed to spill downwards as decaying vegetation.

The wooden beads were added to suggest the 'gone to seed' element and also to break the possible tedium of areas of string. The work was initially intended to hang free but such difficulty was encountered in balancing it on the upper platform that an entire framework with a pedestal base had to be erected, and after attaching the whole form to this it gained a coherent unity. See figures 40 and 41.

39   *Design idea for* Growth Form
Victoria Clarke

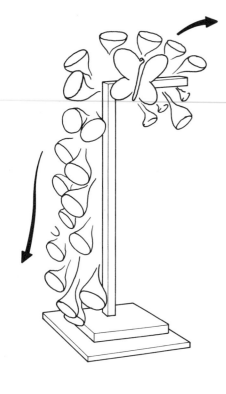

40 *Diagram of framework for*
crochet structure, Victoria Clarke

41 Growth form *Victoria Clarke.*
Dyed string, wire and wood for base.
Crochet. Approximately 2 m
(6 ft 6 in) high

Anna King uses fibre, usually horsehair, goat hair or wool, using the same method, crochet, but bending it to her own angle of vision, creating strange 'beasties' and growth forms, moulded fungi and lichen. There is a very clear path from her inspirational source to its realisation. She says that she arrived at her crocheted forms through a project on vegetable dyes worked on during the summer term at art school. As a result of three months spent gathering weeds, mosses and lichens to use experimentally, she did many drawings of plants (again lichen and fungi predominated) and enlarged them to a grand scale. Deciding how they might best be translated into a textile medium, crochet seemed the right answer. The technique can be freely adapted and the hook is a convenient tool that can be used at any time in any place. She keeps in store a wide range of yarns, as sometimes the yarn itself will suggest a form. She uses unusual contrasts, sometimes six or seven different yarns in any one work. Her preference is for silk, mohair and metallic yarns but she dislikes man-made fibres. Two of her most interesting works shown here are *A hair divides the false and true* for which the design idea arose from a freak mushroom found to have three stalks; and *Lichen 3* where the idea came from lichens of the *parmelia* family. This work was crocheted on a very small hook so that the fabric would be sufficiently firm to hold its shape without padding or wiring, thus achieving sculptural qualities without such aids. See figures 42 to 46.

42   Lichen III *Anna King.*
Hand spun yarn in green,
yellow-green, olive, brown and dull
orange. Crochet. 38 cm × 24 cm
(15 in × 9 in)

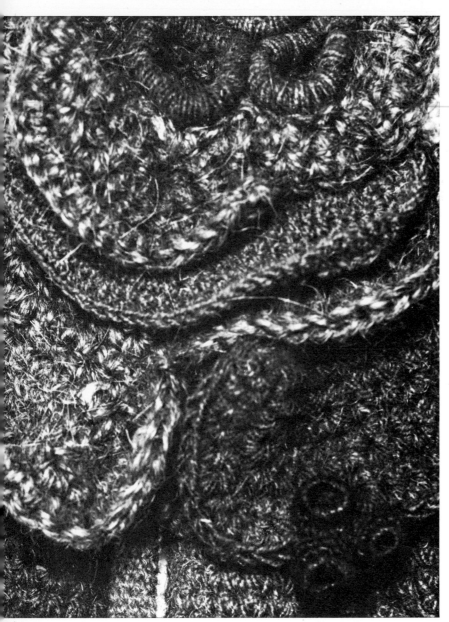

43 *Detail of* Lichen III

44 A hair divides the false
and true *Anna King.*
*Natural wool and hair yarns spun
from goat, camel hair and wools.
The frond-like fringes are of unspun
jute. Crocheted in different sized
hooks. 78 cm × 43 cm (30 in × 17 in)*

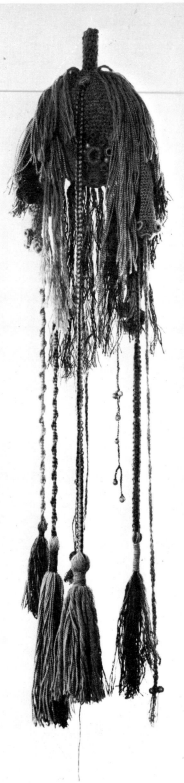

45 Hell, the shadow of a soul
Anna King.
Dark brown horsehair, charcoal and
black wool. Crochet.
90 cm × 38 cm (2 ft 11 in × 15 in)

46 'and two dozen red beads
please' *Anna King.*
Red and purple wool and linen.
Crochet

Almost everyone must be familiar
with the basic stitches of knitting
and crochet. The innovations on
these shown in the illustrations
result either from variations in size
of needles or hooks, the increasing
or decreasing of stitches, changing
type and weight of yarns, or simple
manipulations of thread.

Diagrams of basic stitches are
shown, but for those who are not
acquainted with them, it would be
worthwhile practising them before
attempting any experimental work.
See figure 47.

47 *Method for making double
crochet*

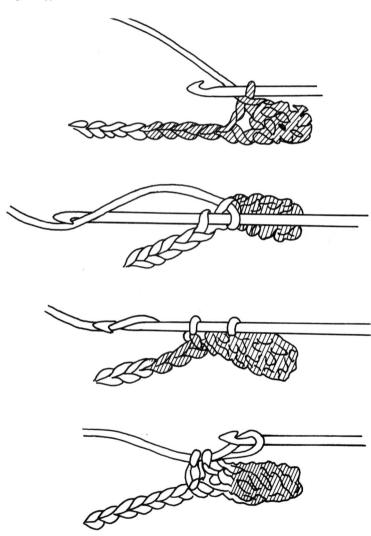

Knotting and macramé

The term *macramé* probably stems from an Arabic word which referred to the ornamental fringes that decorated battle tunics, and was later used to describe a richly patterned form of knotting. Knotting certainly preceded weaving in the important part it played in the everyday life of early man, and the decorative aspect of it came considerably later, breaking away from pure functionalism to create richly embellished articles. Before weaving was thought of, knots were an essential part of man's existence. He tethered his animals with a knot, he knotted the fish hook on to the line and he knotted his nets into a meshwork. He also needed knots to bind and secure canoes, set snares, lash together huts and clothing. He probably used as the only available cord thongs of leather or twisted knotted lengths of grass, flax, animal sinews or vines.

It was inevitable that ornamentation should develop as the years went by, and the decorative knotting of the Arabs became so famous that it eventually spread across to the west; carried to Italy by the Crusaders who brought prized examples to Northern Europe, and then across the Mediterranean into Spain. Soon after the discovery of the New World, macramé work was accepted by the Mexicans, the Peruvians and the North American and Canadian Indians with enthusiasm. The tradition is very much alive today and fine examples of the craft come from these parts.

For some time knotting remained the more functional application of the skill until with the coming of sailing ships, it developed into a maritime art. Sailors whiled away the long months at sea inventing countless variations and embellishments on their everyday knotting tasks. The names of many knots may be traced to these days: reef knots to reef in a sail, bottle and bag knots to make handles for carrying, and the timber knot to secure a rope to a plank with speed.

A wide assortment of cords and ropes were used for the various purposes including sisal, hemp, flax and fishing line, while among the numerous articles of common use were bell ropes, sea chest covers and handles, table cloths, capstan wheel and binnacle covers – all decorated with ornate knotting.

Many more yarns are available now, although the natural ones – hemp, sisal, jute, cotton, wool and linen – are still the most commonly used and probably the easiest to work with, being more pliant and supple. Camel hair, horse hair and goat hair are also used. A wide range of synthetic yarns includes nylon, polypropylene twines, rayon, paper string and waxed seating cord. Some of the more fibrous yarns are rough to handle and better worked with gloves on.

The basic element to be considered in designing is the *Knot* and it is the repetition of this which creates either an ornate surface pattern or a sculptural art form. The examples shown in this book aim to highlight the latter – thus form and scale are ranked above surface embellishment and technical skill. Note that most of the outstanding works illustrated are done in variations of the half hitch which gives great structural rigidity, or in repetitions of the square knot over large areas. It might even be unreasonable to call it *macramé*.

There are at least two approaches to designing in this medium. Some will prefer to allow their imagination to control the course of the work, taking into account the tactile and visual qualities of the yarns that they are using and basing their design on the freedom of movement it seems to demand. The final work may bear little relationship to the original idea as the knotting will have proceeded unhindered by technical restrictions.

Margaret Brown, an artist–craftsman who had been experimenting in knotting for a very short time, making only small samplers, was enthusiastic about attempting a three-dimensional work. As her work began in rather tentative stages, it could be interesting for a beginner in this medium to read her description of these early stages and how she broke away completely from her initial idea. This is described in her own words in a later passage.

In the second approach, the whole scheme is carefully planned beforehand, sometimes on graph paper, and transferred to a squared and numbered board. Quantities of yarn should be measured out before the work starts, and it proceeds within this framework.

Three-dimensional knotting can be done in several ways. To produce a rigid form, several cords can be brought together closely and then knotted to make a stiff column. Free-standing forms are best knotted over and then downwards from a wooden or wire hoop. An example of this kind of work is shown in *Folly*. See figure 48. Here the whole work was structured around seven circular hoops – this method of working is described and illustrated later in this section. An alternative method is to knot over a framework, and when it is finished spray it with several coats of a resin or polyurethene varnish. When these are dry, the framework is removed.

Texture should be considered. Yarns with a complex texture do not always suit the natural knotted surface. Contrast in the actual scale and weight of the material used is of importance, and also helpful in that it can create either (or both) fragility or rigidity within the same framework.

48   Folly *David Price and Jill Pennell.*
Natural sisal. Worked entirely in square knot. 3 m × 2 m (9 ft 10 in × 6 ft 6 in)

Dyeing

A brief section on the dyeing of yarns (which is also applicable to those used in any of the other techniques) is included in this section.

Most of the material used in woven structures is found in natural shades of white, cream, grey and many browns ranging from amber to chocolate black. Sufficient contrast of tone should be possible within this gradation. The mixing of strong or strident colours usually strikes a discordant note. Many of the vegetable dyes will give lovely muted colours. An artist in weaving, Wanda Malinowska, collects pine cones, spruce, bracken, mosses, lichens and many other natural dye materials from her native Polish forests to tint the yarns that she uses. Chemical dyes can be almost as subtle if the directions are carefully followed and the colours occasionally blended with a minute addition of brown or black to mute them. On the whole, strongly opposing

colours affect the balance of form in a woven structure. Exceptions occur to every rule however, as for example, Tadek Beutlich's *Bird of Prey* which is of striking colour contrast and an outstanding instance of an artist's dramatic and imaginative handling of it. See figure 109.

On the practical side of dyeing quite a few technical as well as aesthetic problems can arise. Cottons and linens are easy to dye and generally accept the required tones without difficulties. Chemical dyes are easy to procure and use and I would strongly advise the beginner to start with these.

For all types of dyeing, wind the required quantity of yarn into a skein and tie it loosely in several places to prevent tangling. Soak thoroughly before putting it into the dyebath to enable it to absorb the dye properly. Experiment first with a small quantity of yarn in an equally small amount of dye.

Different dyes are used for wool and the procedure, requiring mordanting, is slightly more complicated. It is not really difficult, however, if the instructions accompanying the dyestuff are followed.

Other problems may arise with plant fibres such as jute, hemp and sisal. Some of these are less porous than others and have to be very thoroughly soaked. Other yarns of short staple and loose twist tend to disintegrate unless carefully tied. The synthetic yarns are usually non-porous and require special treatment. Dyestuff suppliers are given in the suppliers list while textbooks on dyeing are listed in the Bibliography.

Basic materials

These are minimal and are available to anyone at little cost. For a planned macramé piece, you will need a knotting board, upholstery pins for holding the design in place, scissors and yarn. For free working you will need either a strong holding cord, rod, rings or a hoop on which to start the work and, of course, yarn. A board to knot on can be made from any substance that will take the holding (upholstery) pins; insulating board or surplus packing polystyrene are ideal as are upholstery foam or strong corrugated cardboard. Cork is probably best, and old bath mats are sometimes available. Sawdust cushions were used in earlier times but the main requirement for knotting is a vase that suits you and is soft enough to take the pins and firm enough to hold them. A holding cord is stretched horizontally across the top of the board and the knotting strings are attached to this. See figure 49 for the method of securing them. All the work is done from this holding cord, and the vertical strings attached to it must be kept under some degree of tension by holding, tying or weighting the ends by some means that will keep them taut.

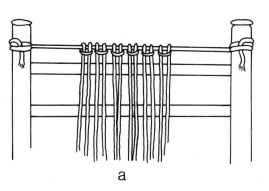

a

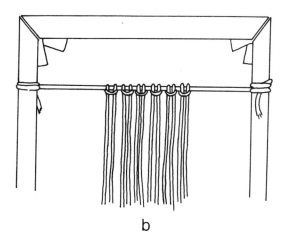

b

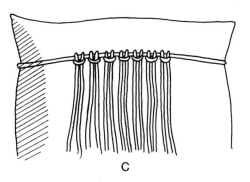

c

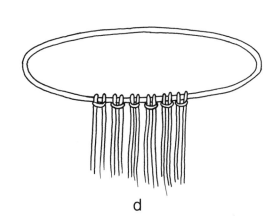

d

49 a *Methods of tying holding cord*
to posts of a chair
b *Holding cord tied across frame*
or canvas stretcher
c *Holding cord pinned across cushion*
d *Holding cord tied from wire*
or cane hoop

For most types of knotting the strings should be in units of four ends, two lengths folded in half and knotted on to the holding cord with a setting–on or lark's head knot. See figure 50. If these strings are numbered from 1 to 4, the centre ones, 2 and 3, are known as the bearer cords and perform a similar function to the warp threads on a loom, the working knots being passed to and fro between them. For some knots, notably the square knot (known also as the flat knot, the reef knot or soloman's knot) these working lengths will be used up considerably faster than the bearer cords; in any case approximately eight times the estimated length of the finished work will be required. Joining the cords is not so difficult in the thinner yarns but almost impossible to do tidily with heavy cords and rope. See figure 51.

The square knot and the half hitch which are the basic knots used in structural knotting are the only ones that will be described in detail.

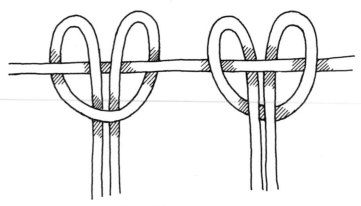

50   *Setting on or lark's head knot*

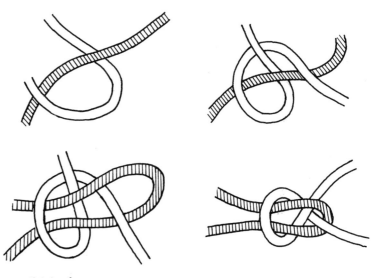

51   *Joining knot*

58

The square knot

The two central cords in this combination of four, the bearer cords, must be kept taut and steady by some means as mentioned earlier. Cords 1 and 4 do the knotting while cords 2 and 3 remain stationary throughout; 2 and 3 therefore are the ones to be kept under tension. Study the diagram in figure 52 before doing the knot. Hold the cords 2 and 3 with the left hand and with the right hand pass cord 1 under 2 and 3 and over 4. This routine is then worked from right to left, taking cord 4 and passing it across 2 and 3 and through the loop on cord 1. Draw this up tightly before forming the other half of the square knot. Now pass cord 4 over 2 and 3. Pass the end of cord 1 over 4, under 2 and 3 and through the loop of 4. Draw this up tightly to complete the knot.

The half hitch

This can be tied vertically, horizontally or diagonally. To make a horizontal half hitch, starting from left to right, cord 1 becomes the knot bearer, placed in front of the other cords. This cord must be held taut – a bit higher than the horizontal. See figure 53a. Cord 2 coming from underneath is looped twice round the bearer cord in two half hitches and continued in this way round each bearer cord. This

method is commonly known as blanket stitch when used on fabric. It is advisable to work a row or two of horizontal half hitch before setting on the cords from the holding cord to give a firm foundation.

The vertical half hitch is made when the knot bearing cord and each subsequent cord become the knot bearer in turn and always lie flat on top of the knotting cord. This knotting cord must be extra long. See figure 53b. When other cords become necessary they can be laid in during the working and threaded in afterwards.

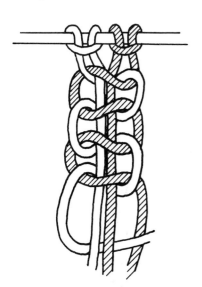

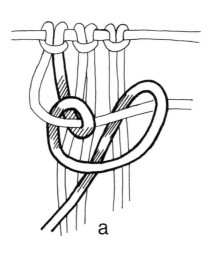

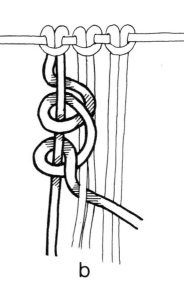

52 *Square knot*

53 a *Half hitch knot – horizontal*

b *Half hitch knot – vertical*

The diagonal half hitch is similar to the horizontal one except that the angle of cord 1 varies according to its position in the design. Decide on the angle wanted and mark it on the board. Keep the bearer cord grasped tightly at the marked point in each successive row, see figure 53c.

c Half hitch knot – diagonal

The half hitch forms the basis of cording, which is the most common routine in macramé work. It consists of double half hitches knotted over a foundation cord known as the *Leader*, which, as described, may be horizontal, vertical or diagonal. Together with the square knot this forms the basis from which most variations spring. Both knots should be practised until they can be done completely automatically. Learn to use both hands and never hesitate to undo a knot that is incorrectly tied.

Sennits
These are knotted braids, usually made by working a series of square knots. Figure 54 shows a spiral sennit, worked by tying a half square knot repeatedly but always starting from the same side, placing cords 1 and 4 over the centre filling cords, 2 and 3. As the braid begins to spiral do *not* attempt to turn the twist but do the knotting on both sides. Many variations of these sennits are done but they are generally incorporated within a larger form. See figure 55 for flat sennit.

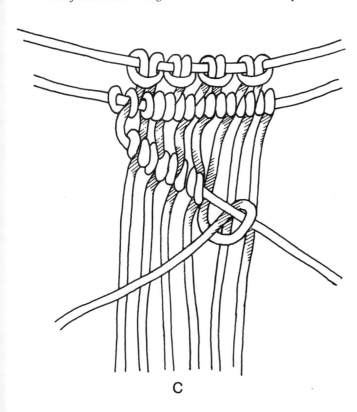

C

54　*Spiral sennit*

Carrick bend or Josephine knot

This is a fancy ornamental knot and may have few uses in three-dimensional work. Any number of cords can be used and the knot is worked with two groups of these laid flat. It is best done on a level plane and pinned into place as the work proceeds to preserve the curvature. A hard flat cushion is good to work on. It is helpful to practice with two contrasting colours while learning the twisting sequence. Make a large loop with white yarn, pass the black over this loop, under the end and over the next section. Gently tighten and repeat. See figure 56.

56　*Josephine or carrick bend knot*

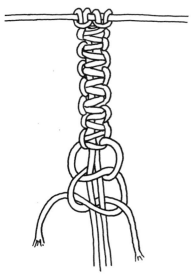

55　*Flat sennit*

Turk's head

This is a similarly decorative knot but sometimes useful in three-dimensional work when made on a large scale, as it can be used flat or as a ball. Follow the directions of the arrows shown in the diagram in figure 57 when forming the three loops as they must be pinned to lie flat in place, and the cord must follow the same journey each time the looping routine is repeated.

To make a ball, the cord must be pushed gradually along its length until it forms a rounded shape. This knot should be worked on a similar base to that of a carrick bend.

Braids and plaits

Braids are primarily based on simple knots, usually half hitches or a series of square knots. They are similar to sennits but generally worked flat. Plaits are not true knotting, more a type of finger weaving, but are often combined with areas of macramé knots.

57   *Turk's head knot*

58   *Plaiting*

Joining the knots

The most common method of forming the knots into a fabric is by joining a series of square knots. Tie a line of cords into a row of square knots as shown in figure 59. In the next row of knotting, lay aside the first two rows on the left, take up the next four cords, ie last two of the first knot and first two of the second knot, leaving the final two cords unworked. Continue in this way, tying square knots across the row. The third row is a repetition of the first row, using the same cords for the square knots. To form a close mesh fabric, knot the rows close together but for an open fabric, space the knots further apart.

The point was made earlier that elaborate virtuoso knotting can so disturb a surface form as to make it meaningless, so a few knots only are described here. The decorative possibilities can carry you away and you are liable to become interested primarily in a labyrinth of knotting. Perhaps one should advise: learn all the knots that interest you so that you can be aware of what should be ignored.

Several interesting examples of macramé used in three-dimensional forms are described and illustrated, showing how individual artists, some working with simple techniques and others with great technical skill and imagination, created their structures.

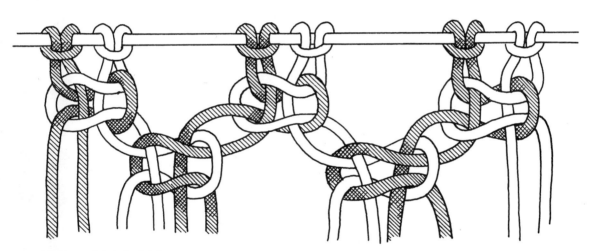

59   *Making a fabric by joining the square knot*

Margaret Brown, mentioned earlier, describes her progress: 'When I first started this work, I intended to make an ornate circular form, possibly a choker necklace, so I pinned a circle of thick holding cord on to a squared knotting board in the size I envisaged... I used white parcel string and brown cord but I now think that it was a mistake to interrupt the knotting surface by using such contrasting tone. It can be seen in figure 60, that the work evolved in a series of half hitches, not at all as I had planned and that the measured squares were ignored after I had set the central circle on them. Figure 61 shows the detail of the half hitch clearly.'

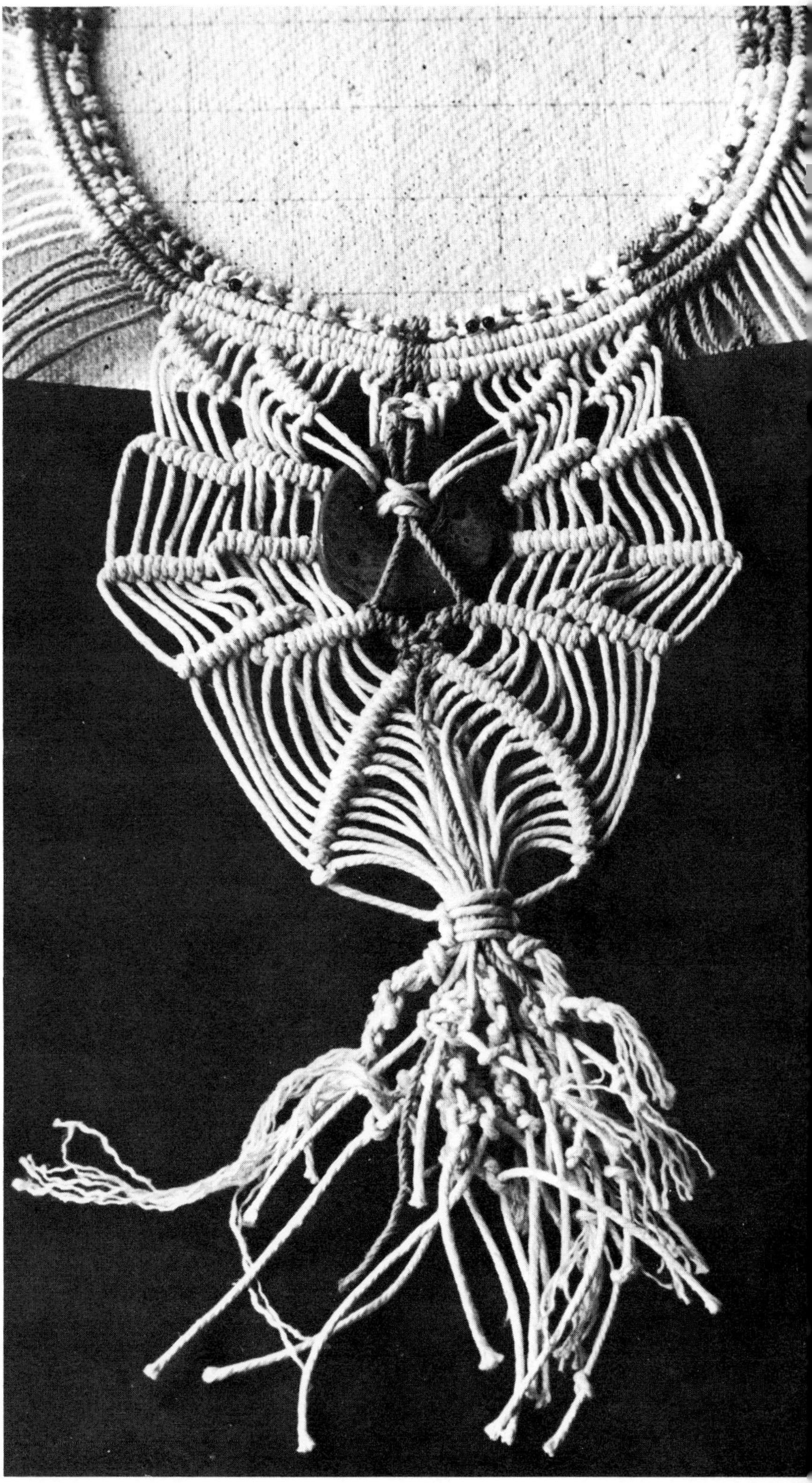

60 *First design attempt, Margaret Brown*

61 *Detail of figure 60*

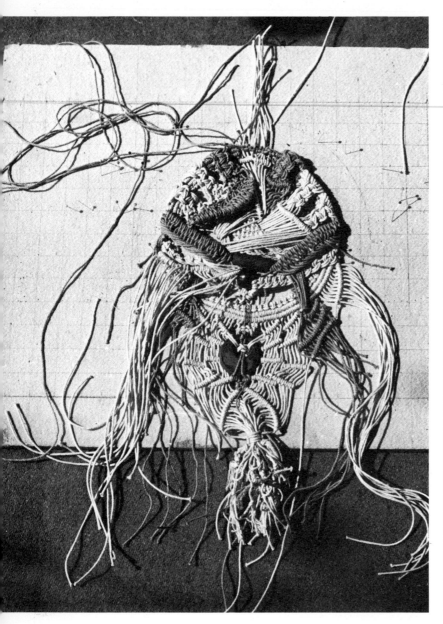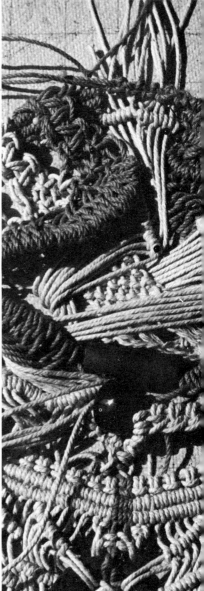

'In figure 62 the whole conception has changed and the knot moves across the surface as infilling, using the half hitch and the square knot in their variations to form a design of tubular sennits and stressed strings. Still adhering to the pendant form, the circle gradually became an ovoid. Figure 64 shows the finished object, the ceramic beads now forming the centre point. Throughout the work, I tried to keep the balance between the two outer perimeters, as I structured the centre. The types of knot and where they were used is shown clearly in figure 63.'

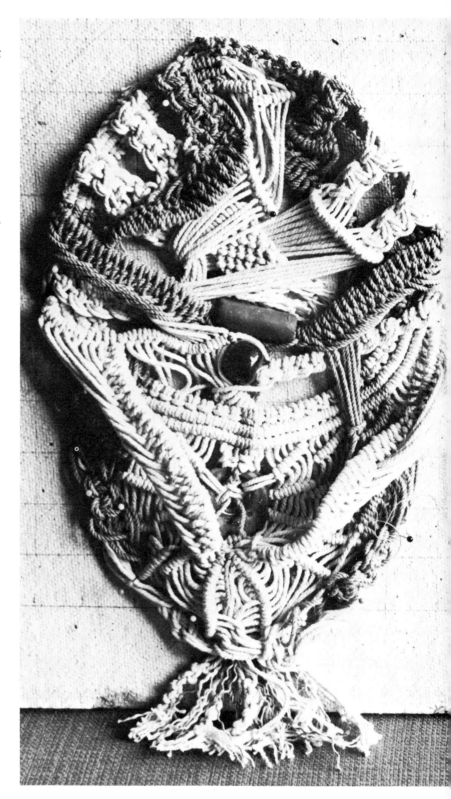

62   *Work in progress, Margaret Brown*

63   *Detail of figure 64*

64   *Finished macramé work, Margaret Brown. White parcel string and brown cord. Knotted in square knot and variations of half hitch. 36 cm × 20 cm × 50 cm (14 in × 8 in × 2 in)*

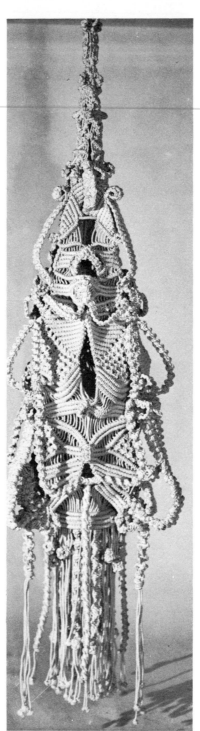

65   Ginger flavoured water
*Fiona Macalister. White string.
knotted in variations of half hitch.
61 cm long (2 ft)*

66   The Tower of Zardeth Zuh
*Fiona Macalister. Thick white string.
Variations of half hitch with some
square knotting. 2·1 m (6 ft 10 in)*

The three works by Fiona
Macalister were also unplanned but
were done by an artist who had
been working in the technique of
knotting for some time. She
describes her work as follows: 'The
design for *Ginger flavoured water*
. . . was not planned and I had no
idea what the final form would be
when I started. I just began at the
top of the first wire ring and
worked downwards, deciding on
each section as I came to it. The
wire rings controlled the shape and
these were added as I thought
necessary. It was worked basically
in the half hitch with variations.
The medium is white string as I
dislike using any colour in
macramé.' See figure 65.

'In the *Tower of Zardeth Zuh* again
I started from the top, deciding on
each piece as I came to it. See
figure 66. I had hoped to knot this
firmly without the wire supports
inside, but later these proved to be
necessary as the heavier string I
had used caused the work to sag
so badly that I had to insert metal
triangles to make the structure
rigid. This was again knotted in
variations of the half hitch with a
few sennits in square knotting. The
Unfinished piece was built up
entirely in one knot – the horizontal
half hitch, commencing with
crossed sennits varied with
diagonal and vertical cordings. It is
self-supporting and shows the
working method of tying the string
in many small bundles to prevent
tangling.' See figure 67.

67   Unfinished piece *Fiona
Macalister.*
*Thick white string, Horizontal half
hitch beginning with crossed sennits.
Approximately 14 cm (5½ in)*

68   Beyond the Sea of Marmora
*Fiona Macalister. Tapestry wool.
Woven on a tapestry loom.
1·1 m × 55 cm (3 ft 7 in × 22 in)*

69

The two examples of the work of Anna King were also freely worked and demonstrate the use of several kinds of yarns. String, horse-hair, camel-hair and goat-hair are all used in the *Panel with a tassel* which in its design and contrasting tone is distinctly Peruvian in flavour. The *Small macramé panel*, made of unspun sisal bound in parts with cotton, has a fragile formality which weds happily with a coarse, inelegant yarn.

69 Panel with tassel *Anna King. String, camel hair, horse hair, goat hair. Flat and spiral sennits, cording and square knots. The design was unplanned. 1·5 m (4 ft 10 in) long*

70 *Detail of* Panel with tassel

71 Small macramé panel *Anna King. Unspun sisal bound around with cotton. Horizontal bound tubes are incorporated into the work. Knotted in half hitch cording with various flat and spiral sennits ending in heavily fringed cotton base. 38 cm (15 in) long*

David Holbourne was originally a tapestry weaver but soon abandoned this craft in favour of non-woven three-dimensional structures. He experimented with rope forms using half hitches, braiding, netting, crochet and weaving techniques to build up these sculptural forms. Becoming increasingly aware of the potential of twine and rope, he sought and used the most direct and least restricting techniques – those that required little equipment, often only a sacking needle. A period of trial and error followed, during which he encountered examples of similar techniques in museums exhibiting traditional crafts. He saw the half hitch knot being used widely in ceremonial costumes from the Congo area, in hats and masks and shoes from various parts of Africa and Polynesia, and masks and fetishes from Pacific Islands. See figure 72.

Five rings is made from natural-coloured lengths of rope spliced into rings and then covered either with whipping or half hitching. Here again the strength of the rope and the firmness of the knotting bring about the rigid form.

72 Five rings *David Holbourne.*
Natural coloured rope.
Rope is spliced into rings
covered with half hitches.
31 cm × 31 cm × 31 cm (12 in ×
12 in × 12 in)

Cartouche knotted by Enid Russ, is a free-hanging form and a good example of the use of synthetic fibres worked sympathetically and effectively. Most of her forms are hand woven and a short description of them appears with accompanying illustrations in the section on weaving. This knotted hanging is set on an oval wooden frame, and is made of white bonded nylon twine and green *Ulstron* polypropylene twine. The work is knotted throughout in variations of the half hitch; the simplicity of the form is stressed by the use of one type of knot.

73 Cartouche *Enid Russ.*
Nylon and Ulstron Cord.
Variations on the half hitch

Folly, a huge knotted work made by two art students, was structured round seven circular hoops of mild steel, the centre hoop being the largest with a diameter of 2 m (6 ft 6 in), the other hoops becoming increasingly smaller towards the top and bottom. The rope used was ordinary 13 m ($\frac{1}{2}$ in) sisal, enlarging to 18 m ($\frac{3}{4}$ in) in some parts. This work was constructed in a back garden on ropes slung between two outbuildings to support the upper hoop which was suspended from this. The second hoop was hung a measured distance below and the rope, after being cut into appropriate lengths, was tied on and knotted down until the next hoop was reached. In this manner the top half of the work was built. The bottom half was carried out in the same way and when this was completed, the two halves were lashed together.

The initial idea for the *Folly* was a sphere with a framework of both horizontal and vertical hoops, but with transportation difficulties in view (it was intended for showing in a major exhibition) the students decided to make it on horizontal hoops only so that it could lie flat. Also, although the size was intended to be only 2·1 m (7 ft) high, the weight of the ropes knotted between the hoops stretched it to nearly 3·6 m (11 ft) in total depth. This is one of the unpremeditated happenings that can occur when working on a project of such large scale. The final result was an eliptical form and another example of the successful use of simple unit knotting. See figure 48.

74 *Example of several knots showing the lark's head attached to the holding cord, followed by a row of half hitch cording. The square knot is joined together to form a fabric. After another row of half hitch cording the simple half hitch is worked alternately from left to right to form chain. Another row of cording is followed by the square knot worked diagonally. Loosely worked half hitching appears in the next large section while diagonal half hitching begins to appear at the bottom of the illustration*

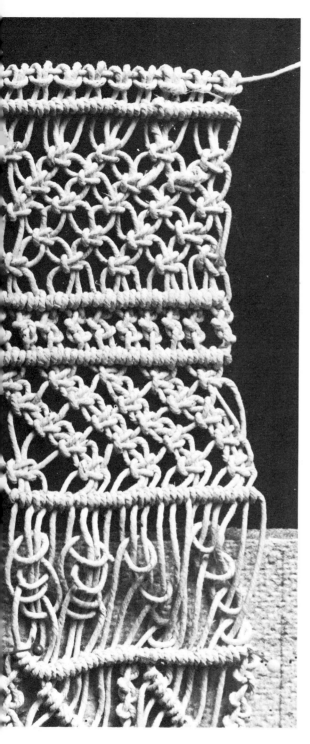

75 *Sampler carried out in diagonal double half hitch in heavy jute dyed deep purple and blue*

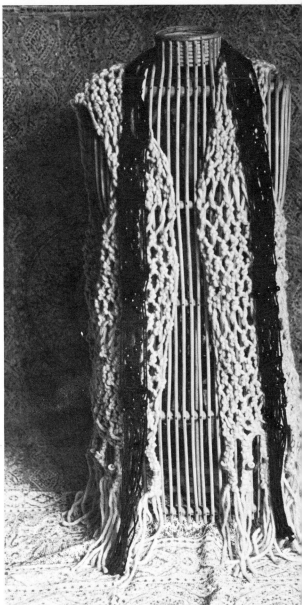

76 *Sampler in natural jute set on brass stair rail. Separate sennits in square knot and spirals hang on each side. The remainder is worked in variations of the square knots, half hitches and some Turk's heads at the top. Ceramic beads are added*

77 *Jacket in cream rug wool shows alternating half hitches with square knot sennits used as a fringe*

Weaving and wrapping

Weaving is a craft of the most remote antiquity and, no one knows at what stage in his development primitive man discovered the means of interlacing fibres. The Saxon word for weave is 'wefan' and the German word 'weben' relates to a woman who works at a distaff and makes a web. It is amusing to read in a Victorian Encyclopedia of Needlework that since the invention of the power loom in 1757 'handweaving is now confined to cloth produced by felons in gaol' thus speedily disposing of it!

Despite the power loom and the felons' monopoly, handweaving is very much alive today. Although if some of the more traditional methods are being discarded or deflected towards new forms, more technically sophisticated or more basically primitive, the end products are imaginative and creative.

Look closely at a section of woven material and you will see that it consists of two sets of threads interlaced crosswise as in darning. The lengthwise threads are known collectively as the 'warp' and those running from edge to edge are called the 'weft'. The interlacing of these threads constitutes orthodox weaving and in this most simple form it is known as tabby weave.

In this book, it is not possible to include techniques involving draft reading and pattern designing with the related complex thread-up of the warp on a multi-shaft loom. Titles of books on weaving may be found in the bibliography. Some of the more simple methods are described, mainly variations on the tabby weave and basic tapestry (interlocking) techniques, and it should be possible to create some of your own innovation from these. Most of the works illustrated are those of skilled artist weavers and are technically too complicated to interpret for an inexperienced beginner, but should be stimulating.

The same types of yarn as are used in other interlocking methods are suitable for weaving, but in this field colour plays a rather more important part. You may prefer to dye your own shades, following the instructions given in the *Knotting and Macramé* section.

Branch weaving and wrapping

This is a useful exercise in three-dimensional work, which gives an understanding of shapes and planes by making use of the contours made by nature. Use branches of a flexible type, with three or more forks. Willow is one of the best as it is reasonably pliable, but many other possible varieties are to be found in woodlands, forests or hedgerows. These skeletal forms, wrapped round with a covering yarn emerge as cohesive structures. Wool, preferably mohair, is a good covering thread, as the fluffy, loosely spun texture clings to the twigs better than cotton or the more slippery synthetic cords. It also swathes more effectively. Sometimes it is necessary to roughen the branch with coarse sandpaper or even notch it if the yarn slips about. Use living wood in preference to dead twigs as they are more likely to snap when under tension.

When a suitable branch is found, wind the yarn into small balls or bundles and tie it at the base of the lowest fork, then start to wrap it crosswise across the rectangular planes. See figure 80. Several decisions will have to be made as to which angles to unite and which spaces to leave open. One method is to start at the base of the first fork and work up the facets created by the need to join the other forks. Variations on the actual methods of wrapping can be invented as it is all fairly haphazard, a no-technique in fact. A three-pronged triangle can be wrapped with three different colours or tones of the same colour across each triangular plane. Or the yarn could be woven down through the warp wrapping, using a large upholstery needle as a shuttle. There are many possibilities.

78 *Example of branch wrapping in cotton yarn on the fork of an apple tree. 38 cm (15 in) high*

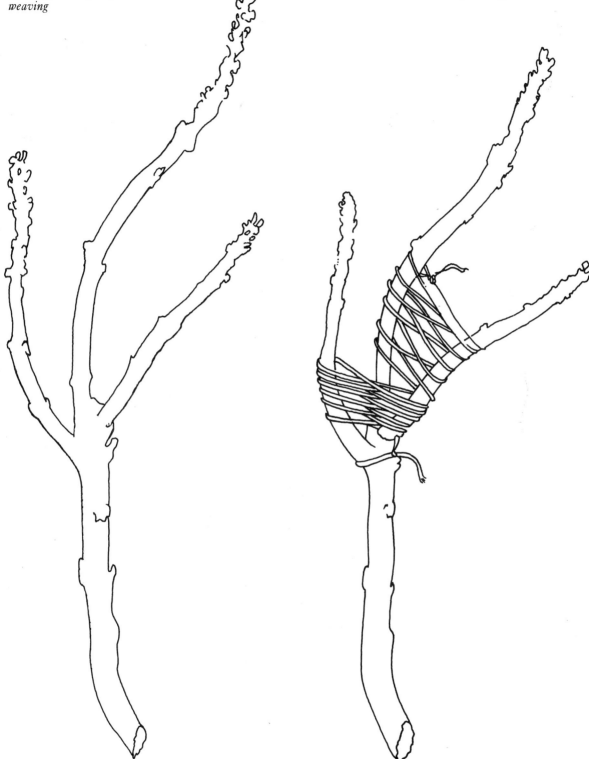

The frame loom

The most simple form of loom for both traditional or experimental weaving is the frame or tapestry loom. This can be home-made in any size and will meet most of the needs of the beginner and many of those of the professional. The large woven works of Wanda Malinowska, were made on such a loom built on a scale to make such creations possible. More complicated tapestry looms, fitted with pedals and other devices on a horizontal or upright frame, are the ones most commonly used by professional weavers working on two-dimensional tapestries. For our purposes, however, the frame loom is quite adequate.

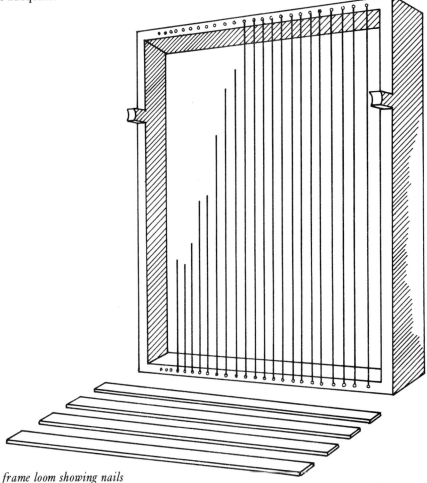

81 *Simple frame loom showing nails for spacing warp and wood battens*

This loom (see figure 81) is built on a rectangle to whatever proportions are required. Alternatively, a sturdy picture frame or canvas stretcher may be used. A canvas stretcher can be bought at any artist's supplier. It has wooden tensioning devices at each corner which are useful for keeping the weave taut. If, however, an old picture frame is used or a home-made frame, the corners should be reinforced with metal angles to provide rigidity. Nails should be placed across the top and bottom at a ratio of eight to 25 mm (1 in), or for a coarser weave four to 25 mm (1 in), to space the warp threads evenly. The spacing of the warp threads, known as the 'dentage' dictates the thickness of the weave. Eight threads to 25 mm (1 in), using medium weight yarn will give a fairly dense weave, while an open dentage of, say two threads to 25 mm (1 in) will give a coarse open mesh. The thickness or fineness of the yarn is also a contributory factor.

Basic weaving method

As the warp threads must be held under tension while the weft is interlaced through them, any system that will keep the threads taut may be called a loom. The warp may be slung over a bar with weights attached to groups of threads at the bottom. A backstrap loom, one of the most primitive types known but still used today in many places, including Peru, Equador and Mexico, is so named because the belt, made of fibre or leather, is attached to a tree and stretches round the back of the weaver who thus controls the tension of the warp with his body.

It is obvious that the frame loom cannot produce a weave longer than the frame itself, and in the more complex tapestry loom a long warp may be rolled round a back beam which is also fitted with a rachet to control its turning. Assuming that a simple frame loom is being used, the next step is the interlacing of the weft threads. This can be done by laboriously threading the weft over and under the warp, one thread at a time. This primitive process is still used with beautiful results by, for example, the Navajo Indians in North America. The accepted method today is to pass each warp thread through short lengths of looped string called *heddles* or *leashes*. Heddles are attached to a

bar which, when raised lifts every alternative thread. In tabby weave, this process is known as making a *shed* and enables the weft to be carried right across the width of the warp with one throw of the shuttle. When the weft is broken up into areas of design, the heddles are grouped together and gathered into bundles called *leashes* which can be lifted by hand, enabling separate pattern areas to be worked individually. *Heddles* are short lengths of cotton twine knotted so as to form three loops. The top and the bottom loops are slipped over a heddle holder or shaft and the warp threads passed through the centre loop. Ready made heddles may be bought or they can be made easily on a simple jig consisting of four nails driven in line into a piece of scrap wood. See figure 82. The use of a jig ensures that all heddles will be exactly the same overall length and size of loop, although the actual dimensions are immaterial. A suitable length would be 255 mm to 305 mm (10 to 12 in). The actual loop carrying the thread has to be in the centre and about 13 mm ($\frac{1}{2}$ in) to 25 mm (1 in) deep. Leashes are merely hand-operated simple string loops, but must be of uniform size.

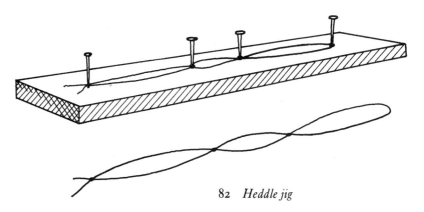

82 *Heddle jig*

Laying the warp on a frame loom

Choose if possible a linen string for the warp and calculate the number of threads as follows: to weave an area for example, 460 mm (18 in) in width for an experimental piece, spread the warp threads at eight to 25 mm (1 in) dentage. Multiply eighteen by eight which will give a total of 144 threads. Add 4 extra threads for selvedges, laying two doubles on each edge, making a total of 148 threads. The length woven is of course, dependant on the length of the frame unless a tapestry loom is used. Check that the warp is centred by measuring from the middle outwards and halving the threads, which will give you 79 each side of centre, the two threads on each edge being double. Wind the warp up and down the spacing between the nails.

To make a shed

Take a smooth, flat wooden batten of about 50 mm × 7 mm (2 in × $\frac{1}{4}$ in) and of the same width as the frame and thread it through each alternate warp thread. This creates the first shed. Now take a thinner round stick with holes pierced in each end and pick up the alternative threads on leashes. The batten and the stick enable you to change the shed. To do so, stand the flat batten on its side, thus raising half the threads through which one row of weaving is to be done (see figure 83). To make the next shed, raise the rod with the leashes. To make this operation easier, brackets fitted on each side of the frame will support the rod, keeping the shed open while the row of weaving is done. As an alternative, single leashes tied in groups of, say, twelve are employed instead of the rod, these are raised in turn, the weft yarn being passed through as each group is raised. This is the better method for experimental work when different sections are to be built up or slits are included in the design.

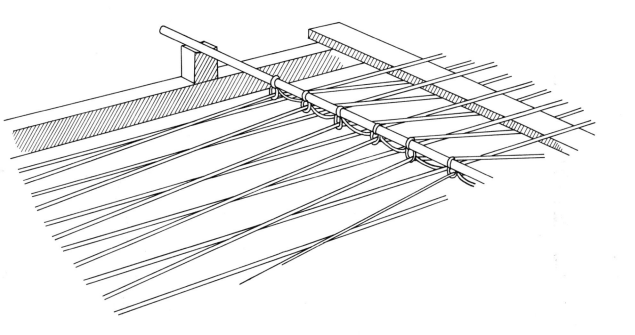

Always weave a few rows before beginning the fabric proper to make a firm edge. If the weft is to be close and dense as in tapestry, it must be well pressed down with a beater between each row. See figure 84. In all types of weaving it is essential to lay in the weft yarn loosely – if it is strained tightly across, the weave will soon take on a waisted effect, so keep a check on the selvedges for straightness. To ensure against a bad edge use a template which can be brought from a weaver's supplier. This is an adjustable metal rod with pronged claws at each end which exert outward pressure on the work.

Weaving

The general procedure is to pass the weft yarn backwards and forwards between the two sheds, raising each one as described, passing the yarn across, either by shuttle or by hand, closing the shed and opening the next one. Joining the yarn is done by overlapping the two threads to be brought together in the same shed, leaving projecting ends to be sewn in later.

Interlocking techniques

Some knowledge of these is necessary if you want to work areas in different tones or colours, or in completely different textured yarns. The Khelim method of interlocking is the one most commonly used and is not difficult to learn. The essence of this technique is the joining of broken areas of pattern in the weft. The yarn is not carried through from selvedge to selvedge in one unbroken thread, but only as far as the edge of the pattern change, when a different yarn is introduced to work across the new area. This thread is passed from the pattern edge and interlocked round another thread as it is introduced. On the return row, the same yarn sequence is used again but in the reverse order until the pattern area is completed. This might take up many rows, repeating the procedure in each one until the design is finished. See figure 85 for the Khelim interlock method.

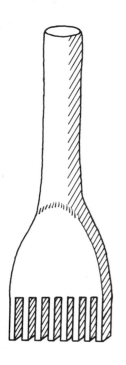

84   *Beater for pressing down weft*

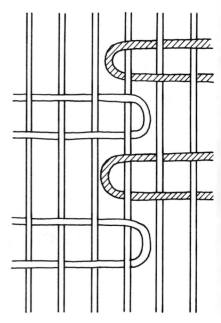

85   *Interlock technique ; Khelim method*

The slit technique

Open the shed and bring the two
different weft yarns from opposite
directions to a meeting point and
to the surface of the warp. Change
the shed and take both weft yarns
back to the original edge again,
using adjacent warp threads as
turning points. At the point where
these two yarns meet, an opening
will be left between two warp
threads and as the weaving
progresses in this way the opening
will become a slit. See figures 86
and 87.

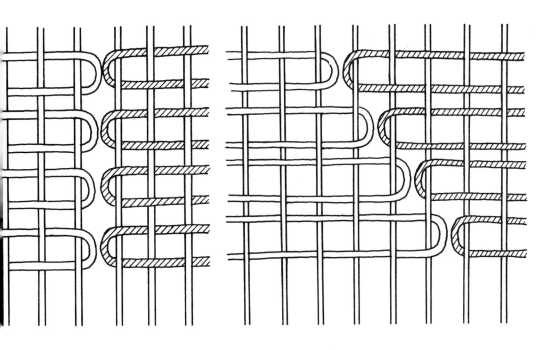

86 *Slit technique*   87 *Diagonal slit technique*

Moulding and shaping

Background threads forming rounded and conical shapes may be built up and moulded with the fingers, pushing threads higher or lower in the weft. Outlining threads in contrasting colour may be used to emphasize shapes.

Dovetailing

This is done by running several wefts of one design backwards and forwards in alternating sheds, from one side of the warp then from the other. The same or different thread may be used for the interlocking.

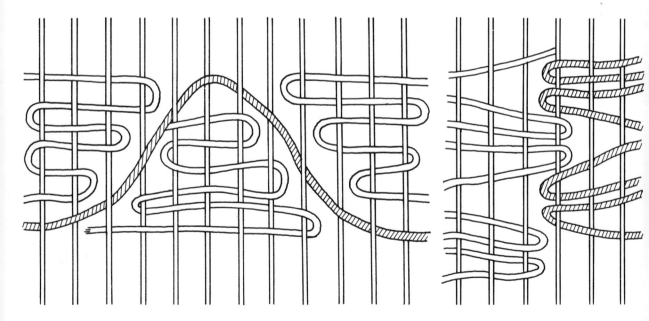

88 *Moulding and shaping technique*

89 *Dovetailing technique*

Tufting

This is always carried out in conjunction with a woven foundation of tabby weave, ie several rows of tabby between each row of tufting which gives the required strength to the background. There are several methods of tufting, all having one thing in common – the tufting must never be carried out on the selvedge edges. See figure 90 showing a method for making the tufts.

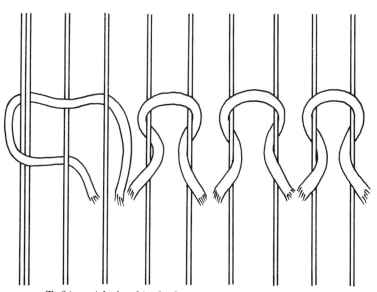

90 *Tufting with the ghiordes knot, showing the method for dealing with a selvedge*

Cut length method of tufting

This consists of knotting cut lengths of yarn into the warp, each length being wound round two warp threads, leaving the ends of the yarn to project on the surface and so form tufts or pile. If areas of even pile are wanted, the tufts should all be cut of uniform length and this is best done by means of a gauge. Make one by fastening two strips of wood or hardboard back to back, winding the yarn round them without overlapping and then slicing along the edge between the double boards with a razor blade or scissors. The total depth of the wood strip must be half that required for the finished tufts. See figure 91.

Knotting method

Knotting is simple. Place one of the cut lengths of yarn over two warp threads, bring the ends round underneath and up again between the two threads, giving a sharp tug to tighten. This makes the Turkish or Ghiordes knot which takes its name from a famous weaving centre in Asia Minor. Other knots are the Soumak and the chain stitch which are not described here, as the Turkish knot fulfils most of the requirements for experimental or three-dimensional work. Do the tufting in a closed shed. Open the shed and do a minimum of three rows of tabby and then close the shed and do another row of tufting. Finish the row with tabby, change the shed and continue in this manner, checking on the selvedges as in interlock technique. You may want to tuft only certain areas and as these parts will then be thicker; they must be compensated for by some extra tabby on each side of it.

Overtwist knotting

This is a useful method to employ when unspun fleece or fibres are used as the weft material. The weft is passed down between two warp threads and to the left, then brought over both threads to the right, then back in between them again and carried under the batten, which is sized to the desired width. The weft is then thrust between the next group of warp threads and thus a loop is formed which can be pulled or puffed up if you wish. These loops can also be cut but the technique is only possible when a complete run of the same colour is planned. See figure 92.

A choice of interesting materials is available for these techniques; spun fleece, teased or unravelled sisal, jute or wool. You may use them in many ways, tufted or overtwisted as described, or covering three or more warp threads as a loop or as an overtwist.

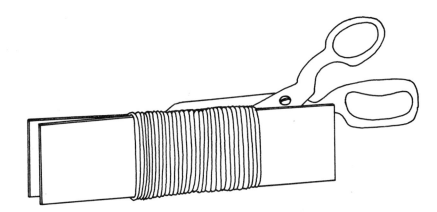

91 *Tufting gauge*

Gauze weave

Gauze weave, in its simple form, consists of twisting two warp threads around each other and securing them with a weft thread. A small pick-up stick and a flat shuttle must be used. Start by weaving a few rows of tabby, then begin at the right side of the work and open the shed so that the first warp thread is on the bottom. Push aside the first thread off the top with the pick-up stick and pick up the first thread below. Keep this on the stick while you go over the next thread on top to pick up the next thread below. This makes the twist. Continue with this process to the other side of the warp. Now turn the pick-up stick on edge so that it creates an opening between the twisted threads and guide the shuttle through this opening, securing the weft yarn at the beginning so that it will not pull through. Remove the pick-up stick and beat down the weft lightly and carefully. Change shed and weave

with the same shuttle and weft through this one without twisting, returning to the right hand side of the warp. Beat gently and again change the shed. Repeat the pick-up process from the start. There are several ways of varying this. Groups of threads can be twisted instead of one. Alternatively, in the second pick-up row the warp threads can be divided and other groups picked up. This technique can be combined with shaggy tufting to create strong contrast of textural surface. See figure 93 for simple gauze weave.

Most of these techniques imply that you have to weave within an area bounded by the frame loom. Even if it is fitted with a roller, you are still only able to extend lengthways. But there are alternatives. You can weave several separate sections and lace them together, or if you want to try a large scale work, it is quite possible to lay a warp on part of a wall. Two lengths of wood or poles of the

total required width should be attached to the wall, one at the top and one at the bottom, blocked out at least 100 mm (4 in), as a space between the warp and the wall is needed for moving the hands or the shuttle. The warp can be attached to a loom bar and suspended from hooks at the top and the base so that the tension can be controlled. Alternatively it can be wound round nails inserted across the top and the bottom bars as in the frame loom. If the warp becomes too slack, folded newspapers can be wedged in beside the shed battens (shed sticks). Always start with at least 25 mm (1 in) of tabby weave and lay four warp threads double to form a selvedge at each edge. This, of course only applies to orthodox weaving working right across the warp from edge to edge. If you are making free forms, slits, or triangular shapes, the selvedges are merely strengthened as shown in the knotting diagram. See figure 92.

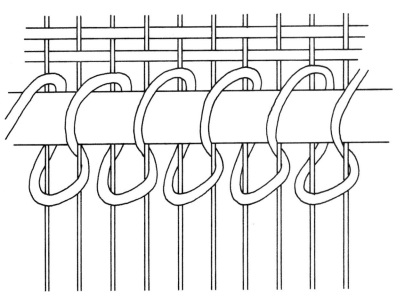

92   *Overtwist knotting*
with continuous yarn

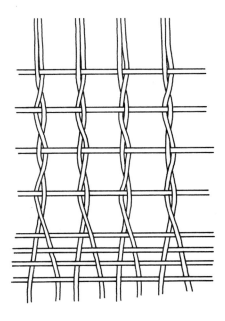

93   *Gauze weave technique*

Magdalena Abakanowicz, who is
internationally known, weaves all
her monumental works by hand
and often uses the free-form and
perforated technique as illustrated.
See figures 94 to 97. Her weaving
grows into great hanging, cloak-like
forms resembling the pelts of
prehistoric beasts. She concentrates
on the texture of the fabric, the
fantastic tangle of the surface,
introducing thick wefts of frayed
cords or rope. She always operates
on a gigantic scale; this is her
special talent. She has a very deep
understanding of the properties of
the materials she uses, integrating
their variety by colour into her
work. After experimenting with
several raw fibres, she chose sisal
as the one most sympathetic to her
purpose and devoted all her time to
three-dimensional weaving.
Although it has been possible to
illustrate only a few of her works,
they all possess the same tendency
to extend their extremities towards
the spectator, the bulk swelling and
oscillating, extending cylindrical

94   Abakan *Magdalena
Abakanowicz. Sisal, wool, hemp,
cotton, horsehair, rope and other
materials. The colours are sombre
bronze, grey, beige, with occasional
flashes of brilliant colour. Weaving
with frayed weft materials
introduced. 3 m × 1·5 m × 1·5 m
(9 ft 10 in × 4 ft 11 in × 4 ft 11 in).
Reproduced by courtesy of the
Arnolfini Gallery, Bristol*

95   Abakan great noir *(foreground)
and* Abakan open *(behind)
Magdalena Abakanowicz. Sisal,
wool, hemp, cotton, horsehair, rope
and other materials. Weaving,
wrapped and joined. The size of each
is 3 m × 1 m × 1 m (9 ft 10 in ×
3 ft 3 in × 3 ft 3 in). Exhibited at
Pasadena Art Museum, California*

arms or fins, sometimes sharp
spikes wrapped in rough sisal fibre.
In a recent statement she said: 'I
am interested in weaving methods
only to the extent that I require it
as a technical means. I have simply
found a material that fits my needs
and imagination.'

A few further comments on her
approach to designing are
significant. Summarised they are as
follows: 'Creating, I use woven
material and string, these
components allowing me to
construct different forms. On the
surface that I make with threads
every square inch differs from the
next as in the creations of nature. I
am interested in constructing an
environment for man from my
forms, and in the scale of tensions
that arise between the various
shapes that I place in space. I am
interested in the motion and
waving of woven surface and every
tangle of thread and rope which
may present the possibility of
transformation. I am totally
uninterested in the practical
usefulness of my work'.

96   *Detail of* Abakan round
Magdalena Abakanowicz. Sisal in
shades of black and brown. Tapestry
weave. Projections of introduced
weft materials. 3 m × 1 m (9 ft 10 in
× 3 ft 3 in). Photograph by Marek
Holzman

97   *Detail from* Rope environment
Magdalena Abakanowicz. Natural
rope in various thicknesses. Knotting
and wrapping. 120 m (131 yd) long.
Photograph by Jan Nordahl

Another Polish artist working on a large scale is Wanda Malinowska. See figures 98 to 104. She has exhibited widely in Europe and recently in Scotland. Having worked in the experimental Tapestry Studios of Polish Artists in Warsaw, she feels that group work is important only in relation to discussions of problems and sharing equipment, and insists that all creative work must be carried out in complete solitude. She says: 'In my tapestries I try to follow a general idea about art – the way we look and feel about the world is what matters. I have never been attached to any particular technique but once I have decided on the one suitable for a particular work, then I stick to its rules'.

98 Gypsy dress *Wanda Nowakowska-Malinowska. The warp is of medium weight linen string, the background weft is natural wool with the web in hand-dyed gold and pink. Woven on upright tapestry loom, using only the fingers. 2 m × 1 m (6 ft 6 in × 3 ft 3 in)*

99 *Detail of* Gypsy dress

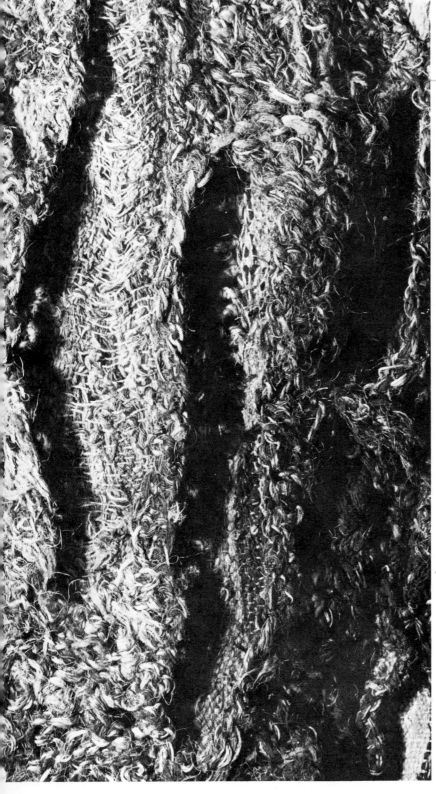

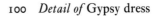
100 *Detail of* Gypsy dress

101 Red shadows *Wanda
Nowakowska-Malinowska. The
warp is of medium weight linen
string. The weft is mainly sisal
mixed with wool, some fine linen
single strand thread. The colours
(which are vegetable-dyed) range
from orange flame, terracotta to
violet. Woven on a wood tapestry
frame loom, the warp stretched from
nails spaced to a dentage of five
threads to 25 mm (1 in). Although
stretched at some tension, sufficient
slack was allowed to enable the
weaver to manipulate wavy sections
with the fingers. Densely woven
areas were beaten down with a heavy
wooden fork. 10 m × 10 m
(11 yd × 11 yd)*

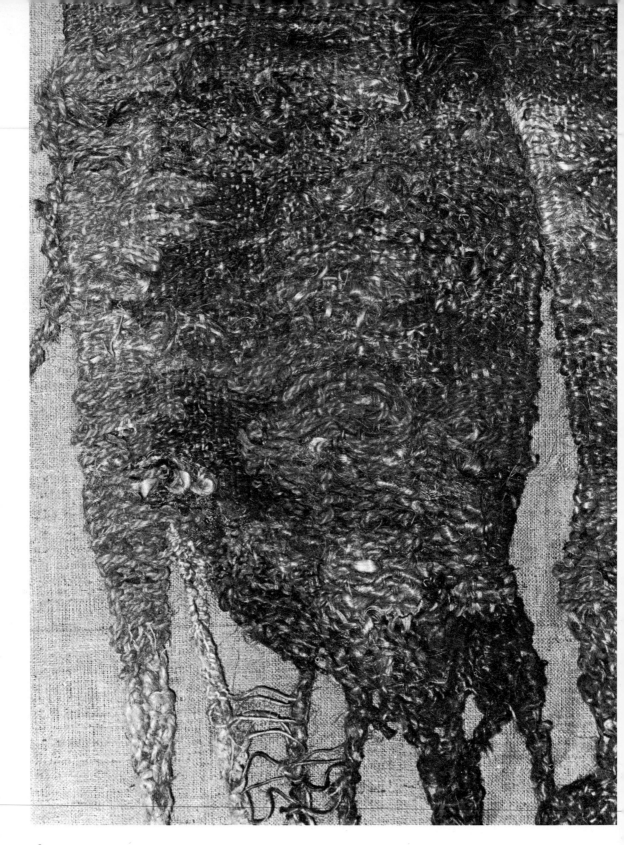

102   *Detail of* Red Shadows
(central section)

103   Foreign planets *Wanda
Nowakowska-Malinowska. The
warp is of fine linen string. In the
weft the central form is of dark
brown wool surrounded by light
coloured cotton rope. Frayed sisal
occurs beneath the dark centre form
while outer edges are red-bronze.
Woven on an upright tapestry loom
vertically, but designed to be hung
horizontally. 2·7 m × 1 m (8 ft 10 in
× 3 ft 3 in)*

The technique practised by Enid Russ has developed from her study of the behaviour of yarn in cloth structures, and her design ideas spring from such skeletal forms as fins, the rigging of ships, sails, basketwork and the rib cage. Her three-dimensional weaving is done on a horizontal 96 cm (38 in) loom, equipped with four shafts and six pedals. The pedals are tied in such a way as to enable her to weave in two superimposed plain cloths which can be readily exchanged from the upper to the lower cloth. The *Big Insect* was woven in such a way with the cane crossing from one layer to the other to form intersecting planes which fall into place when the piece is hung. See figure 106. It hangs from a single thread so that it turns freely, giving varied patterns seen through the canes and from the light-catching and reflecting Flectafoil. *Crosshatch* is woven in narrow strips linked in varying ways by areas of bristle. See figure 105. The strips are knotted into a wooden disc suspended by a thread. The bristle links displace them out of the vertical and create tensions. The lower ends are weighted by rings.

104 *Detail of* Foreign planets (*central section*)

105 Crosshatch *Enid Russ. Yellow and white cotton twine warp, cotton weft and bristle. Woven on a four shaft loom in narrow strips, linked in varying ways by passages of bristle. The strips are knotted into a wooden disc suspended from a thread. The bristle links displace them out of the vertical and create tensions. Lower ends are bound on to rings for weight. 1·4 m × 46 cm (4 ft 6 in × 18 in)*

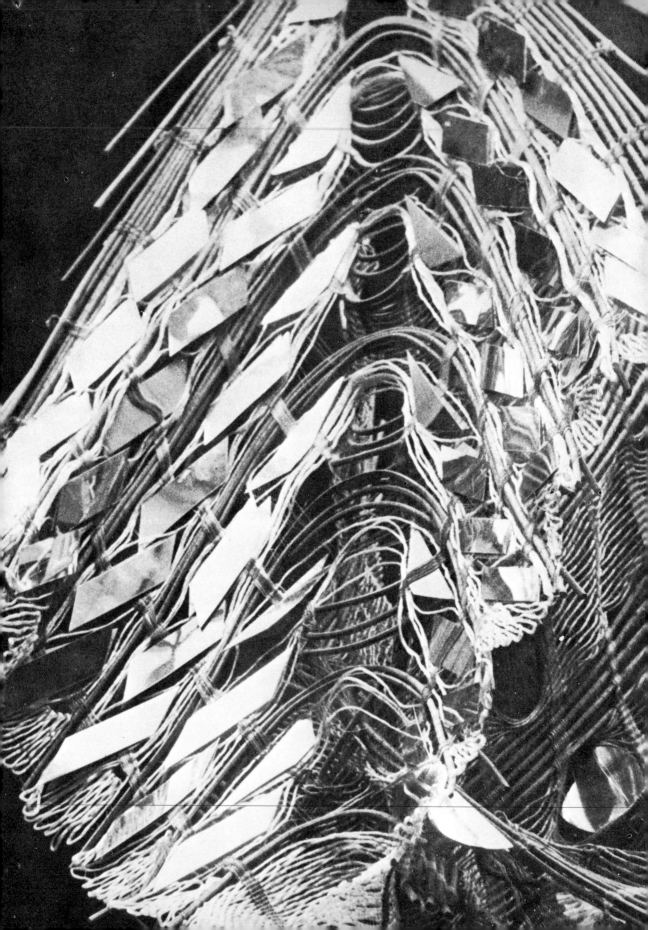

Enid Russ uses many different weft materials to provide colour or decorative elements, including saturated pliable cane incorporated in a rib structure. Complex structures are formed and when the work is hung correctly and the cane dry and firm, tensions develop, pulling the forms into rigid shapes, often helped by the addition of weights in significant places.

Tadek Beutlich was formerly a painter, then a tapestry weaver, and his hauntingly atavistic fibre sculptures have taken on their present form in answer to the strong need he felt to be able to touch and feel his conceptions. See figures 107 to 109. Most of them are woven in jute, sisal, mohair nylon or a combination of all of them, while the type of weave is generally the overtwist knot. He dyes his weft materials with Coomasie ICI dyes. The main impact of the work is brought about by the switch of techniques: the smooth tabby weave breaking forth into knotted protruberances, sometimes cascading into tousled, fraying fibres. In other compositions he uses fringed unravelled fibres. He designs and works on a large scale, anything between 6 m to 12 m is not uncommon, and size contributes considerably to the significance of his works.

107 Moonworshipper *Tadek Beutlich. Sisal. Woven, knotted, overtwisted. 1·8 m × 2·1 m (6 ft × 7 ft)*

106 *Detail of* Big Insect, *Enid Russ. Dyed cotton warp. Cane weft with various yarns and coloured* Flectafoil *insets. Woven on a four shaft loom as a double cloth with the cane crossing from one layer to the other to form intersecting planes which fall into place when the piece is hung*

108 Icarus I *Tadek Beutlich.*
Sisal and nylon frayed yarn.
Tapestry woven, knotted,
overtwisted. 2·1 m × 1·8 m
(7 ft × 6 ft)

109 Bird of Prey *Tadek Beutlich.*
Sisal, jute, mohair, dyed with
chemical dyes. Tapestry woven,
knotted, overtwisted. 3·6 m × 1·5 m
(12 ft × 5 ft)

The work of Ted Hallman, a Californian, is well known in the USA and in Europe. His approach to three-dimensional work is simple and very direct, the forms evolving as a result of the struggle which emerges when taking elements from a two-dimensional plane out into a third dimension. He dyes and often bleaches out his yarns, tearing away parts of a work and re-making it until the final concept comes into being. His *Handwoven mask* woven over a moulded metal form, is made in handspun wool and linen fibres; the colours are natural with shades of rust, grey and purple. See figure 110. The other work illustrated *Interlaced tree* is a cobweb-like form in the section on knitting. See figure 24.

Kay Sekimachi, another well-known Californian artist weaver, shows work in a sophisticated and beautiful form of structural weaving, which she calls *Monafilament hangings*. See figures 111 to 113. The tubes evolve naturally from card weaving in its simple form, woven on either four or six hole cards. The weft is entered from the same side and after being woven, is pulled in to form a tube. In the *Monafilament hangings*, the design is planned beforehand, the weaves being double, tubular and multi-layered. The work leaves the loom on a flat plane, a plastic ring is inserted in the tubular part and the work opens up to take on another dimension. The tube or strip is hand-manipulated to make its final form.

The *Maragawas* tubes made of bright coloured linen thread fall in straight coils but the fragile *Monafilaments* appear to defy the laws of gravity and to float freely in space. Technically these are beyond the skill of the beginner as they were woven on a loom with several shafts and pedals and a complicated thread-up of warp threads.

110   Handwoven mask *Ted Hallman. Handspun wool and linen fibres in shades of natural, rust, grey and purple. Plain weave over a three-dimensional metal form*

111   Nagare VI   *Kay Sekimachi. Black nylon monofilament. Tubular and quadruple weave*

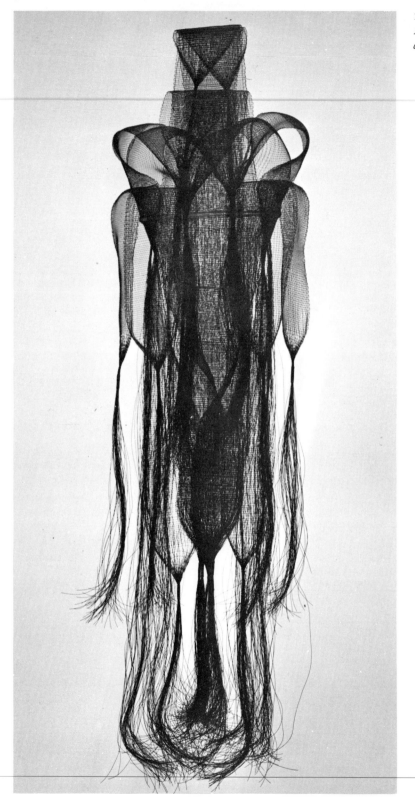

112 Katsura *Kay Sekimachi.*
Black nylon monofilament. Tubular
and quadruple weave

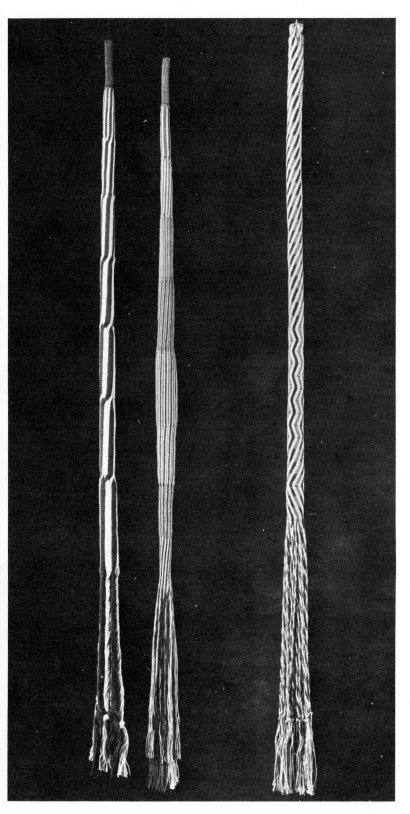

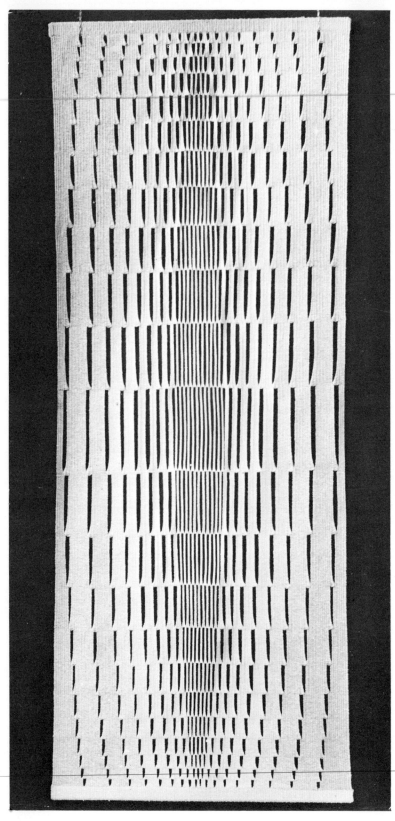

Moik Scheile, who is Swiss and internationally known has worked in the medium of textiles for fifteen years, developing new techniques to give expression to her ideas. See figures 114 to 118. She uses mainly synthetic materials such as aluminium, silver thread, or nylon in different weights. She always weaves three-dimensionally. Technically, her work is brilliant, but she works with such subtlety that the actual technique is never allowed to obscure the design conception. A clear relationship to bas-relief sculpture is evident in her work.

114　Space element *Moik Scheile. Synthetic yarns. Tapestry weave in slit technique. 1·6 m × 2·5 m (5 ft 3 in × 8 ft 2 in)*

115　Woven Waves *Moik Scheile. Synthetic yarns, yellow on yellow. Three-dimensionally woven*

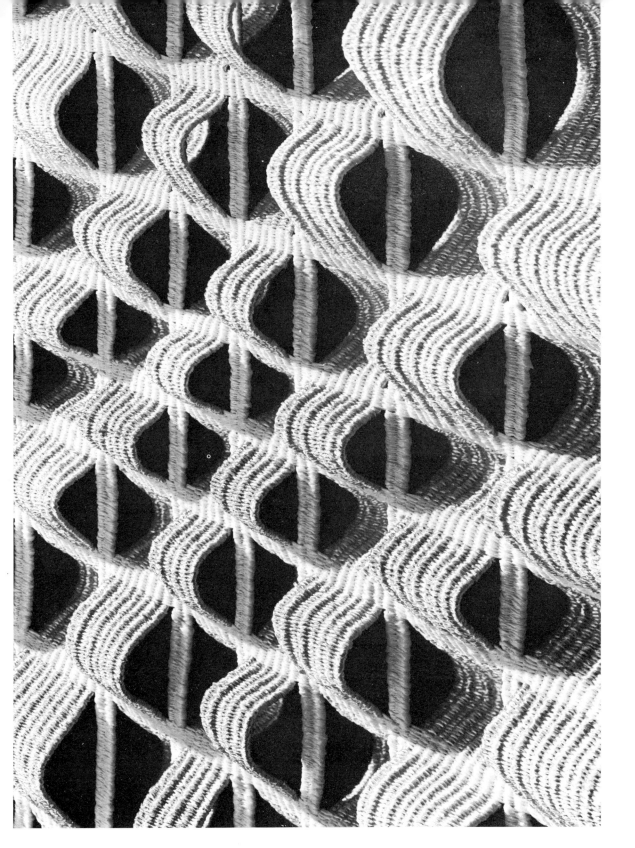

116 Copper Waves *Moik Scheile.*
Synthetic yarns. Three-dimensional
tapestry weave. 8 m × 1·5 m × 60 cm
(27 ft 3 in × 4 ft 6 in × 2 ft)

117 Textile space element
Moik Scheile. Synthetic yarns,
green, blue and purple. Transparent
tapestry weave. From the chapel in
Fiensenbert

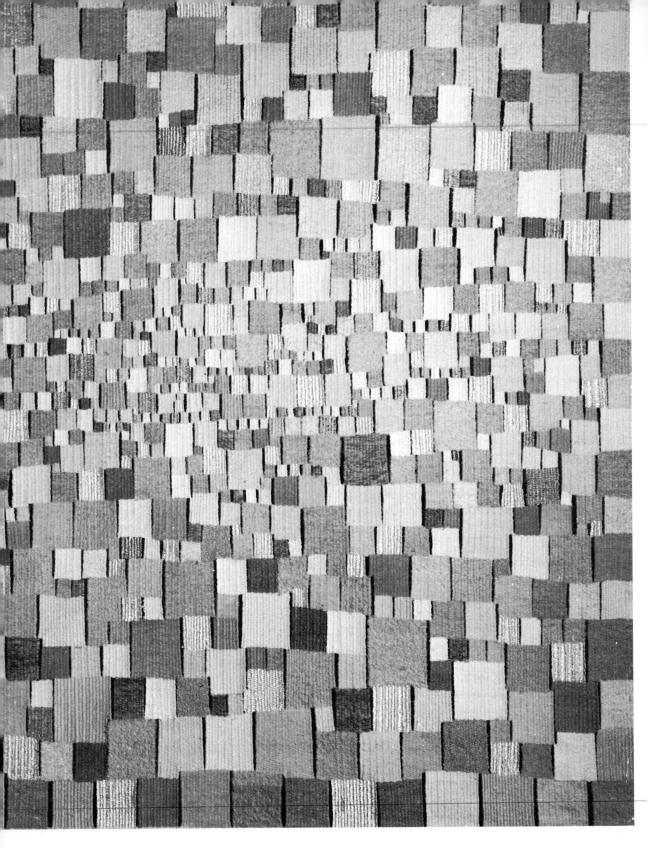

114

118 Textile element *Moik Scheile. Various types of thread in shades of white. Tapestry weave in three-dimensional slit technique. 2 m × 2 m (6 ft 6 in × 6 ft 6 in)*

The works of Eta Ingham-Mohrhardt shown in the two illustrations are significant in that she weaves entirely freely without the draft plan that normally accompanies work so technically complex. Breaking away from tradition, she gives the weft threads waving movements instead of running them at right angles to the warp. She allows broken threads to interrupt the surface and when she finally moves into a third dimension, she manipulates threads into a more strict discipline. See figures 119 and 120.

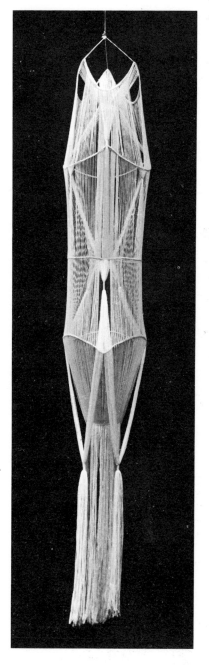

119 Hanging in shades of white *Eta Ingham-Mohrhardt. Natural and white wool. Manipulated threads. 3 m × 80 cm (9 ft 10 in × 1 ft 8 in)*

120 Snowscape *Eta Ingham-Mohrhardt. Wool, cotton, nylon in black, grey and white. Tapestry weaving. 1·5 m × 1·2 m (5 ft × 4 ft)*

Other methods

Rope sculpture

Edith Simon names her works *Ropescapes* and in most cases they consist of one single, unbroken length of rope ranging in length from 30 m to 228 m (25 yd to 200 yd). Each rope sculpture is made from an uncut coil of hemp – other types of ropes such as sisal or nylon could be used. The rope is set up with the aid of supports, strings, pulleys, etc, easily intertwined and twisted into the desired design. It is then coated with three to five layers of Strandglass resin, the thickness of the coating depending on whether the work is for indoor or outdoor use. When the resin has finally set, the 'web' is cut from the moorings, preferably with secateurs, and any remaining bits of string can be pulled off without any risk of injury to the actual composition.

The Horse was made of 137 m (150 yd) of 75 mm (3 in) rope, requiring six to seven coats of resin; the same system of supports and pulleys was used in its construction.

The Crown of Thorns is built similarly and is 2.7 m (9 ft) high.

In designing, continuous line drawings were the first step, exploring form and leading the eye round the picture in one fluid movement. Each drawing consisted of a single line, unbroken from start to finish, which is a pleasant visual exercise to retrace. Invisible masses are caught within the outline with startling plasticity. In the *Ropescapes* there is the same return to the point of departure, carrying the technique of continuous line fully into the third dimension.

121 The Crown of Thorns *Edith Simon. Back view. Hemp. 2·7 m (9 ft) high*

122 The Horse *Edith Simon.*
Hemp rope. Life size

Student work
The following illustrations show
the work of three students.
(Courtesy of Bedford
College of Education)

123 Ruckled Forms *Gail
Bodsworth. Fleecy domett. The idea
for this work was the result of
experimenting with folds and
creases in different textured
materials. The domett was
manipulated into a rucked base and
black tape, looped and twisted along
the folds, was then sewn in place.
The resulting form was a random
pattern from which a dark landscape
mass emerged*

124 Puff Balls *Tess Dexter.*
White stockinet. This was inspired
by fungus growths. The stockinet
was chosen because it gave sufficient
elasticity to allow the stuffing to
form different sized puff balls. Each
ball was tied at the base

125 Hoover Remains *Caroline*
Revitt. Natural unspun brown fleece,
some parts dyed to a deeper shade.
This was finger woven by pulling the
fleece through the thin linen warp

Appendix

Addresses of the World Crafts Council

United Kingdom
British Crafts Centre
43 Earlham Street
London WC2H 9LD

USA
WCC, 29 West 53rd Street
New York City
New York 1019

Argentine
Argentine Section WCC
Rioja 2368
Olivos
Buenos Aires

Australia
Crafts Council of Australia
27 King Street
Sydney, NSW 2000

Canada
Mr G Barnes
Canadian Committee WCC
R R 3, King City
Ontario

Denmark
Miss Dorte Raaschou
Acting Representative
Puggaardsgade 7
1573 Copenhagen

France
M. Jacques Anquetil
Maison des Metiers d'Art
28 Rue du Bac 75
Paris VI

Germany
Mr Nickl
Arbeitsgemeinschaft des
deuchen Kunstandwerks,
Max Joseph Strasse 4
Munich 34

Ireland
Crafts Council of Ireland
c/o Royal Dublin Society
Ballsbridge
Dublin 4

Italy
WCC Seziona Italiana
Via Durini 34
20122 Milan

Mexico
Comite Mexicano pro
Artesanias y Artes Populares
A C Morelas 49
Mexico 14 D F

New Zealand
New Zealand Crafts Council Inc
21 Macfarlane Street
Wellington 1

Switzerland
Section Nationale Suisse WCC
27 Malagnou
1208 Geneva

The World Crafts Directory is now available and may be obtained by members. It lists the principal crafts and craft areas of each country and the names and addresses of organisations as follows:
Government agencies concerned with crafts
Associations of craftsmen
Schools teaching crafts, summer schools and seminars
Museums showing crafts and regular exhibitions
Galleries, shops, native markets and trade fairs
Magazines showing crafts
Information available from Marita Burkhart, Information Officer, World Crafts Council, 29 West 53rd Street, New York City, New York 1019, USA

Suppliers

United Kingdom

Art Needlework Industries Limited
7 St Michael's Mansions
Ship Street
Oxford OX1 3DG
Threads, wools, etc

British Twines Limited
112 Green Lanes
London N16
Twines, etc

Craftsman's Mark Limited
36 Shoreditch Road
Farnham
Surrey
Natural wools

Dryad (Reeves) Limited
Northgates
Leicester LE1 4OR
Cotton and wool yarns, dyes

Thomas Hunter Limited
56 Northumberland Street
Newcastle upon Tyne NE1 7DS
Threads, wools, string, etc

ICI Limited
Digswell Lodge
Digswell Rise
Welwyn Garden City
Hertfordshire
Coomassie dyes – inquiries

John Keenan and Company Limited
64 Little Horton Lane
Bradford 5
*Worsted yarn in two ply,
oiled or scoured*

Linen Thread Company Limited
Hilden House
Parry Street
London SW8
Warp string, etc

Mace and Nairn
89 Crane Street
Salisbury
Wiltshire
Threads, wools, etc

M Matlock and Sons
44 Vauxhall Bridge Road
London SW1
String

Mister Bosun's Locker
East Street
Chichester
Sussex
Cord and ropes

The Multiple Fabric Company
Limited
Dudley Hill
Bradford 4
Horsehair, wool, mohair

Christine Riley
53 Barclay Street
Stonehaven
Kincardineshire AB3 2AR
Scotland

Simpers Ropeworks Limited
New Street
Cambridge CB1 2QV
Rope, natural and synthetic fibres

Skilbeck Brothers Limited
35 Glengall Road
London SE15
Dyes

Southwick and Case Limited
38 Canning Place
Liverpool 1
Hemp, jute, cotton yarns

J W Stewart
Ask Mills
Mussleburgh
Midlothian
Scotland
Netting twine

Uni-dye
Rear Castle Yard
Church Street
Ilkley
Yorkshire
Dyes

USA and Canada

Coulter Studios
138 East 60th Street
New York
New York, 10022
Yarns, threads, wools, etc.

The Mannings
East Berlin
Pennsylvania, 17316
Yarns, weaving supplies

School Products
312 East 23rd Street
New York
New York, 10010
Yarns, weaving supplies

The Yarn Depot
545 Sutter Street
San Francisco
California 94102
Yarns, threads, wools, etc.

Fezandie & Sperrle
103 Lafayette Street
New York
New York, 10013
Dyes of all types

Nature's Herb Company
281 Ellis Street
San Francisco
California, 94102
Natural dyestuffs

Bibliography

Big Knot Macramé
NILS STROM AND
ANDERS ENESTROM
Sterling, New York
(distributed by Ward Lock in
London)

Introducing Macramé
EIRIAN SHORT
Batsford, London
Watson-Guptill, New York

Macramé
VIRGINIA L HARVEY
Van Nostrand Reinhold
London and New York

Colour and Design in Macramé
VIRGINIA L HARVEY
Van Nostrand Reinhold
London and New York

Macramé
DONA Z MEILACH
Allen and Unwin, London
Crown, New York

Practical Macramé
EUGENE ANDES
Studio Vista, London
Van Nostrand Reinhold, New York

Macramé
BETTY ALFERS
Harrap, London

Do Your Own Thing With Macramé
LURA LA BARGE
Pitman Publishing, London
Watson-Guptill, New York

Creative Crochet
NICKI EDSON & ARLENE STIMMEL
Pitman Publishing, London
Watson-Guptill, New York

Beyond Weaving
MARCIA CHAMBERLAIN &
CANDACE CROCKETT
Pitman Publishing, London
Watson-Guptill, New York

The Technique of Macramé
BONNY SCHMID-BURLESON
Batsford, London;
Branford, Newton Centre,
Massachusetts

Knots: Useful and Ornamental
GEORGE RUSSEL SHAW
Ward Lock, London

*Nets and Knots: for Fishermen
and Others*
QUINTON WINCH
Dryad, Leicester
Woodridge, New Jersey

Creative Knitting
MARY WALKER PHILLIPS
Van Nostrand Reinhold
London and New York

*Golden Hands Book
of Knitting and Crochet*
Collins, London
Random House, New York

*Golden Hands Book
of Machine Knitting*
Marshall Cavendish, London

Introducing Knitting
AUDRIE STRATFORD
Batsford, London

New Designs in Weaving
D J WILCOX
Van Nostrand Reinhold, London

The Art of Weaving
E REGENSTEINER
Studio Vista, London
Van Nostrand Reinhold, New York

The Technique of Woven Tapestry
TADEK BEUTLICK
Batsford, London
Watson-Guptill, New York

Card Weaving
CANDACE CROCKETT
Pitman Publishing, London
Watson-Guptill, New York

On Weaving
ANNI ALBERS
Studio Vista, London
Wesleyan University Press,
Middleton

*Spin Your Own Wool,
Dye It and Weave It*
MOLLIE DUNCAN
Bell, London

Weaving is for Anyone
JEAN WILSON
Studio Vista, London
Van Nostrand Reinhold, New York

Simple Weaving
GRETE KROCHE
Van Nostrand Reinhold
London and New York

Card Weaving or Tablet Weaving
ROBIN AND RUSS
Handweavers, McMunneville
Oregon

Off the Loom
SHIRLEY MAREIN
Studio Vista, London
Viking Press, New York

*Encyclopedia of Victorian
Needlework
Volumes 1 and 2*
S E A CAULDFIELD
Dover, New York

Creative Textile Design
ROLF HARTUNG
Batsford, London
Van Nostrand Reinhold, New York

Inkle Loom Weaving
NINA HOLLAND
Pitman Publishing, London
Watson-Guptill, New York

Ancient Dyes for Modern Weavers
PALMY WEIGLE
Watson-Guptill, New York

Textiles: Properties and Behaviour
EDWARD MILLER
Batsford, London

Thread: an Art Form
IRENE WALLER
Studio Vista, London
Viking Press, New York

Lichens for Vegetable Dyeing
EILEEN M BOLTON
Studio Vista, London
Branford, Newton Centre,
Massachusetts

Form and Space
E TRIER
Thames and Hudson, London
Praeger, New York

The Origins of Form in Art
HERBERT READ
Thames and Hudson, London
Horizon Press, New York

Bizarre Plants
WILLIAM A EMBOLEN
Studio Vista, London
Macmillan, New York

Forms and Patterns in Nature
WOLF STRACHE
Pantheon, New York

Vegetable Dyeing
ALMA LESCH
Watson-Guptill, New York

Periodicals

*Quarterly Journal of the Guilds
of Weavers, Spinners and Dyers*
1 Harringdon Road
Brighton 6, Sussex

Craft
28 Haymarket, London SW1Y 4YZ

Craft Horizons
(American Craftsmen's Council
Publications)
16 East 52nd Street
New York City

Handweaver and Craftsman
220 Fifth Avenue
New York City

The Master Weaver
Handicrafts, Fulford, PO Canada

Shuttle, Spindle and Dyepot
(Members of the Handweaving
Guild of America only)
339 N Steele Road
West Hartford, Conn 06117